DATE DUE

MAY 1 1 1999	MAY 0 2 1999	7?
	DEC 0 6 2004	
DEC 2 7 2004		

Demco, Inc. 38-293

THE YOUNG PRETENDERS

The Young Pretenders

A STUDY OF TEENAGE CULTURE
IN CONTEMPORARY SOCIETY

JOHN BARRON MAYS

Second Edition

SCHOCKEN BOOKS · NEW YORK

'. . . the first duty of youth is not to avoid mistakes, but to show initiative and take responsibility, to make a tradition not to perpetuate one.'

R. H. TAWNEY

PREFACE TO THE SECOND EDITION

I welcome the opportunity to write a brief preface to this new edition of my book. First, because when it appeared, some critics made sharp attacks on its contents and upon my own attitudes; and second, because since then some important studies and research reports have appeared on both sides of the Atlantic which make valuable contributions to the ongoing discussion about the nature of adolescents in contemporary Western societies.

Two main criticisms were made of this book which are worth comment. In the first place, I was taken to task for daring to suggest that young people today, as always, need some kind of moral training. As one favourable reviewer, John Highet, put it, writing in the *British Weekly:* 'this is very daring of him, for, of course, to talk this way gets a horselaugh from many of the brash young intellectuals doing reviews and comment in our metropolitan periodicals.' All I can say about this is that I am quite unrepentant and that, while I appreciate the difficulty in finding firm ethical guidelines for youth, I believe that the attempt must be made. Not to attempt to give help and guidance would be to betray our own children and leave them to their own resources at a time when they need us most, and perhaps thereby to imperil the whole, rather wobbly foundation of Western civilization. We may have our doubts about what to do or say; we may detest an overly dogmatic approach; but we cannot, dare not, let the whole matter slide.

A second criticism made by some reviewers was that I underplayed the importance of 'pop' culture and leisure-time entertainment generally. One critic argued that I was trying to present Hamlet without the Prince of Denmark, that I was missing the whole significance of teenage culture as a new form of intercommunication among the young. I can only say to these critics that this book was deliberately not about pop culture as such, although I do discuss certain sociological aspects of this new social phenomenon. But I do not consider it to be of fundamental importance, nor do I think that it has a very deep or lasting influence upon the vast majority of ordinary young people. Its influence is phasic, short-lived and epiphenomenal in spite of the strong commercial interests that have avidly fastened on the growing affluence of the teenage consumer group. I am certain that the three main issues—coming to terms with society, with the self and with life as a whole—which form the main body of this book, are still the basic tasks all young people are obliged to face and that for a very long time to come they will remain so.

Two studies, one in Britain, the other in America, have appeared since this book was written; both are of outstanding interest, and both in their different ways underline many of the points that I have tried to make. Dr. Michael Schofield's *The Sexual Behaviour of Young People* (London; Boston, 1965) was based on a study of 1873 that dealt with adolescents of both sexes between the ages of 15 and 19 who were unmarried and living in the South of England at the time of the enquiry. His findings show that young people today are far from being the sex-obsessed, bored, irresponsible tearaways and degenerates that some less scientific commentators would have us believe. Schofield shows that the momentous years for sexual experience are the middle and late teens and that by this age some 34 per cent of the boys and 17 per cent of the girls had had some sexual experience, although in many cases this fell short of full intercourse. In other words, the sexually experienced young adolescent is still, in Britain, in the minority group. Such a finding may be reassuring to parents as also may be the fact that permissive parents come out poorly in this enquiry.

The Adolescent Experience by Elizabeth Douvan and Joseph Adelson (New York, 1966), based on interviews with some 3,500 boys and girls between the ages of 14 and 16, is also a valuable essay on the general theme of adolescence in modern society. Using the core analytical concept of the self-image, they have shown (*a*) that the key orientation for the adolescent is the future, not the present; (*b*) that boys' vocational goals are not often coloured by dreams of glory; (*c*) that a substantial difference divides masculine and feminine conceptions of respective social roles; (*d*) that boys, because of the necessity of exercising greater independence, are obliged when young to challenge their environment more than girls; (*e*) hence, that girls are less gang-minded or herd-oriented than boys and are more absorbed in interpersonal relationships; (*f*) that there is an apparent homogenisation of

American society in terms of characteristically middle-class values; (*g*) that a democratic home atmosphere is best suited to produce autonomous individuals in later life; (*h*) that there are two adolescent self-images—the masculine and the feminine; (*i*) and that therefore there are two adolescent crises, the masculine and the feminine, which can be clearly demarcated.

These findings of Douvan and Adelson reinforce many of the points I have tried to make in this book. They also tend to come to rather dismal conclusions about the state of contemporary American adolescents. Too few seem to achieve full all-round maturity. Content within the playpen of their peer-group culture, far too many, in the last analysis, seem to forfeit their 'true' adolescence and instead become mere 'teenagers'. If this is so, and I believe that the evidence accumulating is fairly strong, then it is clearly the fault of our social leaders and educators that youth today is offered so poor and stultifying a cultural diet that they turn to pop as to a temporary lifeline. It is because these social facts and trends seem so important and universal that *The Young Pretenders* was written in the first place. If in this new edition it can continue to contribute to the serious examination of such important social problems and to stimulate further discussion and enquiry, I shall be more than satisfied.

Liverpool, 1967   JOHN MAYS

PREFACE TO THE FIRST EDITION

When I decided to call this book *The Young Pretenders* I did so with the *double entendre* consciously in mind. Young people today are, in fact, pretenders in both senses of the word. They are youthful heirs waiting to come into their inheritance. They know that the future is theirs and that the day when they will have to shoulder full responsibility for their own lives is drawing closer. But they are still mere understudies rehearsing in the wings for the parts they will one day have to play on the adult stage. They strike first one pose, then another. They toy with the props to find out what fits and becomes them most; what external façade is most engaging; what stance or swagger attracts the requisite amount of attention.

All this changeableness arises from the transitional nature of their position in society, and it is the continuing uncertainty of role that makes the more vulnerable of them victims of anxiety, frustration and despair, and which also exposes them at times to the intoxicant of an over-bold self-confidence. They can be passive and impatient, dynamic and lethargically inert, doubting yet opinionated, frightened and almost heroic in quick succession. They change from mood to mood with bewildering rapidity. This contrariness makes older people shy away from them or shelter behind a defensive smokescreen of criticism and condemnation.

Such tactics, however, only emphasise the inadequacy of the adult group to deal confidently with a swiftly changing and unfamiliar state of affairs. In the face of hostile and unsympathetic adult attitudes, youth is all too ready to 'go it alone'; to create its own youth culture and live its own life in its own way regardless of the censures of the 'old men'.

Far too many parents simply abdicate at the point when their children reach adolescence. They ignore the problems of youth or, more blandly, leave them to the professionals, the psychologists, teachers and social workers, to cope with. If no competent professional educators are available to give the necessary advice and help the whole business goes by default. As a consequence, a considerable number of youngsters live through their adolescent phase in a condition of spiritual isolation. They have no reliable person to turn to for guidance, no one to discuss things with or whose experience they can tap. They have only their peers to share their anxieties with and when they do discuss serious topics with contemporaries there is often such a degree of tension and anxiety created that what might have been a constructive fellowship evaporates in a mist of banter and embarrassment.

It is not surprising, therefore, that the years between 16 and 21 are often the loneliest in our lives and this is tragically borne out by the fact that the suicide rate for this younger age group has gone up by something like 100 per cent since the end of the second world war.

We will not, I believe, make much progress, either as parents or as educators, until we face up to the fact that growing up in contemporary society is a serious and tricky business. Adolescence is certainly as crucial as early childhood for determining the life-pattern of the individual but it has received much less attention from psychologists and social scientists. The movement from juvenile dependence to full autonomy is an arduous and difficult road. The successive stage points are not reached or passed automatically. All sorts of problems—psychological and sociological, personal and public—arise which make the journey a trying one even for the products of happy well-integrated families. For those who derive from disturbed households the hazards are accordingly much greater. Not only is the track naturally a rough one, there are also a whole number of obstacles set in the path, sometimes by older people, which have to be circumvented.

These latter obstacles exist, in the main, I believe, because we are not quite clear about the nature of our society and the values we ought to uphold. Much hard thought needs to be given to this question during the next decade or so in order that our educative institutions may be enabled to function more harmoniously with other aspects of the social structure. Amongst contemporary writers who have given a lead in this direction the name of Raymond Williams seems to me to be outstanding. If any may be said to be worthy to wear the mantle of the late R. H. Tawney today, Raymond Williams is undoubtedly one of the strongest claimants to that honour.

One of the things I have deliberately avoided in this book is a chapter specifically devoted to a consideration of young people's leisure time pursuits. There are a great many such studies already available and I did not wish to add to the list. This is not because

I regard leisure activities as unimportant—far from it—but because I think, in our general approach to and concern about young people, we often do less than justice to their situation by concentrating attention mainly on what they do when they are not in school or not at work. Leisure and leisuretime activities are important but are not to be thought of, as they so often are, in isolation or disassociated from other and more vital aspects of young people's lives. To concentrate on what individuals do in their free time is to suggest that what they do in their working time is not very important. Hence all I have to say about recreation is woven into what I have to say about their general task of finding their individual identities, first in relation to their own nature, second in relation to society, and finally to what, for want of a better word, we may call 'the universe'.

This book, then, is an essay on the social significance of adolescence. It attempts to grapple with some of the basic problems of training youngsters for freedom and responsibility in the belief that the quality of individuals will greatly affect our future corporate life. Parents and teachers are nowadays in a good deal of perplexity about what to do and how to act. Many notions and nostrums are peddled, some essentially sound, others wildly heretical. They have to be judged against the measure of our fundamental social purposes. What these purposes are and should be I shall try to state but not to argue.

In presenting this work I am conscious of the debt I owe to many other writers and thinkers whose ideas I have freely drawn upon in the text. I hope that the references in the many footnotes will to some extent repay this debt. I am particularly grateful, however, to Dr Mark Abrams for permission to quote freely from his writings and in particular to reproduce a significant table from his booklet *The Teenage Consumer*, and also to Dr W. D. Wall for the inspiration that his work in this field has given me.

J.B.M.

Liverpool, 1965

CONTENTS

CONTENTS

Part One

CHAPTER I YOUTH CULTURE TODAY

1

The current adult image of youth, if we may judge by newspaper reports, is one of comparative irresponsibility, hooliganism and disrespect for established authority. It is a picture which can only be described as a caricature and one which most young people, naturally enough, resent very strongly.

Probably at no other time in the nation's history has there been so much adverse criticism of youth as there is today, and so little understanding, also, of what really is its role and function in society. So much so, in fact, that there is a very real danger of something like inter-generational alienation developing and spreading in the future. If this should happen, the social consequences will be very serious indeed.

Most of the men and women who today occupy positions of power and authority grew up and were educated in a very different social climate from that which the rising generation experiences. The majority of the middle-aged, who are currently at the height of their influence, were born and bred in the troubled twenties or the anxious thirties. They grew to maturity themselves through a series of national crises, economic, political and military, which followed in the wake of a terrifyingly destructive European war. Not only were they accustomed to economic depression and inured to high rates of unemployment at home, but abroad they were faced with the rising threat of Fascism.

The present-day teenagers and younger men and women in their early twenties have little knowledge of such a world. To them such things as mass unemployment, endemic poverty in certain parts of the country, the obscene threat of Nazism, are no more than the legends of the Napoleonic campaigns and the Crimean War were to earlier generations. Those who have not had to live through the bitter years of the slump and of rising unemployment, who have not seen children running barefoot in the streets or known friends or relatives die of malnutrition, cannot be expected to conceive what such things mean to the older generation. We have to remember that today there are many young people who do not recall the last war, who know next to nothing about Hitler or the Nazi extermination camps and for whom names such as Spain or Abyssinia are merely geographical in significance. We have got to accept the fact that, from the nineteen-thirties to the nineteen-fifties, there has been a widespread social revolution also. Our culture has undergone profound changes. Attitudes have altered, sometimes subtly, sometimes drastically.

The generation of ex-service fathers hoped and attempted to make for themselves and for their young families a society which would be free from the dangers and threats which had overshadowed their own youth. Peace in the international field, economic prosperity and security, social welfare and equality of opportunity at home were the immediate objectives that they set themselves to attain. Certain consequences have followed from these decisions. Not the least of these consequences is the emergence of a great many like-minded young people who have accepted and made their own these perhaps limited ideals of security and personal success.

2

It is customary nowadays to speak of a 'youth problem.' Many are of the opinion that something like a rot has set in amongst Western youth. There are, of course, many historical precedents for similar gloomy pronouncements about the state of young people's morals by our ancestors. 'Sinful dalliance' is not a new charge to be brought against young people.

There does, however, seem to be something exceptional about our contemporary adult concern and alarm about youngsters' conduct. Whether this resides in their unusual depravity or is merely an expression of our exceptionally sensitive consciences is an open question. But there is no mistaking the alarm expressed.

In Western Germany, for example, social critics currently speak of 'the sceptical generation' of young men and women, now apparently so disillusioned with their past that many of them are committed to a life of mere banality and egocentricity. Politically they seem to be unnervingly indifferent and generally divorced from the great issues of world and state, or, to use Mulock Houwer's expressive phrase, 'morally freewheeling.'[1] Considerable publicity is given

[1] D. Q. R. Mulock Houwer, Commentary on *Teddy Boys and Teddy Girls*; *International Child Welfare Review*, Vol. XV, No. 4, 1961, p. 221.

to the more flamboyant kinds of teenage behaviour. Television and wireless programmes, books, articles, newspaper reports and editorials highlight each sign of abnormality and almost hysterically drag into the open every symptom of deviance.[1]

One of the inevitable results of all this discussion is growing uncertainty in the minds of parents on the one hand and increasing self-consciousness on the part of teenagers on the other.

It is clear that young people are not only more numerous than they used to be, but they are also much more conspicuous. In different countries there are individual distinguishing marks, quirks of behaviour or sartorial differences which provide an indigenous façade. But the inner picture is essentially the same. Different names (Teddy Boy, *Halbstarke, Leder-jacken, Stilyagi,* and so on) epitomise similar manifestations of a peculiarly reactive juvenile mentality. The semi-delirious addiction to rock 'n' roll and to jiving and other dance forms has taken by storm such apparently dissimilar cities as London, Paris, New York and Moscow. Neither the content nor the spirit of the contemporary youth culture seem to know material or political boundaries.[2]

Playwrights and novelists seem to be especially intrigued by the emergence of the new social group of teenagers. Colin MacInnes in his book, *Absolute Beginners,* has gone further than most sociologists or psychologists have yet been able to do in describing what it feels like to be a teenager in a predominantly teenage milieu. So too, the brash ebullience and undisciplined energy of proletarian youth in contemporary Britain has been perfectly imaged for us in the personality of Arthur Seaton in Alan Sillitoe's widely read novel of working class life in the Midlands, *Saturday Night and Sunday Morning.* His self assurance and assertiveness, his sexual promiscuity and easy-going amorality seem to typify a reaction which is fairly common amongst certain sections of youth today.[3]

There is little doubt that the young heroes—or rather anti-heroes —in the successful novels of writers like Sillitoe, MacInnes, Braine,

---

[1] It is sometimes said that this over-concern about youth's morals is merely an expression of an unconscious or hidden desire on our part to do the very things we condemn in them.

[2] The craze for 'pop' singers has swept across the world and penetrated the seemingly otherwise impermeable 'iron curtain.' Political commentators in East Germany, for instance, have described Elvis Presley as America's 'secret weapon'!

[3] 'Don't let the bastards grind you down. What I'm out for is a good time. All the rest is propaganda!'

Storey and others depict the emergence of a new type of young man in British Society. They are not the prey of gnawing inner uncertainties nor are they overwhelmed by inferiority feelings or class anxieties. The world, or at least a tangible succulent part of it, is their oyster, and they mean to eat it before they die.

It is fatally easy to write off such characters as utterly philistine, barbaric and banal, to treat their somewhat cavalier rejection of established values as a challenge to essential human decency. They are clearly, however, not to be categorised as either misfits or as criminals. They are young men who have found for themselves a new form of social adjustment. They are certainly not 'Teds', although they have been subjected to some of the same influences. They have been the target for commercial exploitation. They have loitered in cafés and coffee bars, listened to juke-box records, hummed pop tunes and tried out the latest dance steps. But they are much more than disturbed or anxious adolescents. There is no hint in them of the introspective morbidity epitomised in the earlier adulation of James Dean. One cannot imagine Arthur Seaton or Joe Lambton committing suicide. They are not rebels in the way that the *Halbstarke* (half-strong) are, fisting off the tyrannical image of their fathers, and refusing in a mood of almost psychopathic infantilism to accept the external world as it is. Rather they are moving towards the culturally classless society of the future which Richard Hoggart has predicted will eventuate as the growing pressures of the mass media and the new educational system affect more and more people.

There is, furthermore, another group of young people, a much more morally committed and politically aligned section, who are deeply concerned by the imminent threat of total annihilation and who are compelled to speak out against the government's fatal acceptance of the hydrogen bomb and nuclear weapons. The main body of those who protested against Polaris submarine bases at Holy Loch or who marched annually to Aldermaston is made up of teenagers and young people generally. I think we will seriously underestimate the significance of such protest marchers if we merely write them off as manifestations of the inevitable dissatisfactions of youth with the world their fathers made. These demonstrations, in my view, have a much deeper social and moral significance. They are a reminder that idealism is not dead but is entrusted afresh to each new generation.

3

One of the many social factors which may predispose adolescents in our society to anxiety, doubt and indecision was long ago mentioned by Margaret Mead.[1] It consists in the amazing number of choices presented to them as, on the threshold of maturity, they begin to assume responsibility for more and more areas of their own lives. The world at this stage of youngsters' development looks more like a gigantic cafeteria or a vast emporium than anything else. The only difference perhaps is that there are no obvious price labels attached to the varying choices so temptingly arrayed. Cost is something that is discovered only by experience and in the end may turn out to be overwhelmingly high.

Youngsters in our culture seem to grow up via a series of minor crises. At all stages decisions are thrust upon them by parents, teachers, friends, the wider society and by the demands of their own bodies and physical constitution. There are examinations to pass, crazes to survive, crushes and love entanglements to escape from, blind alleys to avoid, religious and philosophical doubts to allay, ambitions to pacify and angry aggressive impulses to quell. It is a complicated and sometimes a heart-breaking business.

Other strains generated by the social structure have also been isolated as being especially typical of our own day and age. In the U.S.A., and, to a lesser degree, in Britain, there is considerable geographical mobility amongst the 'rootless' professional and aspirant middle class families. This means that the influence of local institutions and neighbourhood traditions is greatly reduced. That sense of belonging, sometimes thought necessary for the mental health of individuals and families, is, in a frequently changing environment, impossible to develop. Social suspicion and isolation may consequently arise which in turn can foster anxiety and frustration and either result in mental ill health or be deflected into delinquent activities.

Social mobility, mobility, that is to say, between the social classes, can further aggravate the position. The business of passing the class bar may be similar to passing through the colour barrier. Having to accommodate psychologically to different customs and standards of behaviour can prove to be a painful experience. One aspect of this may well be contained in the cant phrase 'keeping up with the

[1] Margaret Mead, *Coming of Age in Samoa;* Penguin Books, 1954, pp. 161–2.

Joneses' if the Joneses are one's new and unfamiliar neighbours and if they are conspicuously the pace setters for consumption standards.

A rapid rate of technological change also characterises the contemporary world. The simpler satisfactions derived from more traditional methods of work have had to give way to automatic processes and repetitive procedures. However, it must be admitted that technical advances are likely to disturb the middle-aged rather than the youthful members of the community. Only perhaps in the modern possibility of high speed, creating as it does an ever increasing hunger to go faster, is youth most obviously affected. Whether the motor bike and the car, which are prominent features in the new youth culture, precipitate or merely reflect a growing hysteria and obsession with danger and recklessness is impossible to determine. 'It is taken for granted', says Professor Jessie Bernard,[1] 'that every teenager will learn to drive and that, if he does not have a car of his own, individually or as a member of a group, he will certainly have access to one.' It is a prestige symbol of great power. James Dean died on the road, it will be remembered, and Françoise Sagan, the young French novelist, had a car crash which added greatly to her emotional appeal for the youthful public. Not only is the automobile an acknowledged instrument for courtship amongst the younger generation, it is also an added inducement to delinquency. Furthermore, the desire to possess a car or bike has become for many youngsters a major motivating force. It absorbs much spare time, grows into a love object and so becomes a constructive influence in their lives.

Greater accessibility to cars and motor cycles, therefore, is seen to be a neutral cultural trait. It may serve to develop hobbies and technical interests; at the same time, in other hands, it can lead to more sophisticated delinquencies and greater public danger and annoyance.

4

Social mobility is, at the moment, mainly of an upward nature. Individuals tend to achieve occupations with a higher status and greater financial reward than their parents. Especially since the pass-

1 Jessie Bernard, 'Teen-Age Culture: An Overview'; *Annals* of the American Academy of Political and Social Science, November 1961, p. 3.

ing of the 1944 Education Act in England, which made secondary education, theoretically at least, available to all without any consideration of means or background, children from the lower economic groups have been enabled to pass the necessary examinations and in increasing numbers enjoy both grammar school and university education. But youngsters who have achieved higher class jobs have often done so at a price. The pangs of the working class scholarship boys have been well described by Richard Hoggart.[1] There can be little doubt that increasing educational opportunities have set rifts between the generations and driven cultural wedges between children and their parents. Social changes, whenever they occur in depth, lead to social disorganisation and produce a fresh crop of problems for young and older folk alike. The faster social changes occur and the more of them there are, the greater the strain generated and the greater the incidence of resultant individual breakdown.

Against this kind of a general background, another feature of teenage life, which will be considered in more detail later on, has occurred since the end of the last war. This is the phenomenal increase in adolescents' earning power and spending. Young people have now, probably for the first time in our history, obtained freedom of action and the economic strength to rebel against any features in the social structure which displease them. They can no longer be ignored as minors or have their desires and claims brushed aside as inferiors. In all income groups and social classes this is manifest, although the changes have been most conspicuous amongst the working class boys and girls at an earlier stage of their development than with their middle class counterparts.

Similarities in the attitude and status of youth are observable and have been reported throughout the whole western world. Undoubtedly these common characteristics arise from common experience. In what used to be the more depressed sections of society, these new conditions have produced a state of mind which seems to be at times self-consciously hostile to the adult world, defensive and even defiant. Modern urban youth, at least a substantial proportion of them, want to look different from the rest of the community. They want to talk, to behave, in a distinctively teenage manner. Only thus, it seems, can they assert their disapproval of the whole adult

[1] Richard Hoggart, *The Uses of Literacy*; Chatto and Windus, 1957: and Penguin Books, 1958.

world which they experience, in spite of their improved economic position, as excessively powerful and frustrating. The common dress and habits, furthermore, act supportively and help individuals to feel conscious of their solidarity with one another which gives them added courage in their struggle for self-assertion.

This is, of course, by no means a novel state of affairs. Inevitably young people must feel themselves at times to some extent in conflict with their parents' values and ways of life.[1] Some kind of rebellion against authority is necessarily involved in the growing up process. It is a prerequisite for the establishment of personal autonomy. What is unusual, however, in both European and American societies today, is the degree to which this hitherto usually benign reaction has sometimes been carried. What is remarkable is the vehemence of the gesture with which it is nowadays necessary for youth to repudiate the middle aged. There are possibly pathological factors at work here, visible in the exaggerated way in which a minority of youngsters flaunt their difference and signal their independence. To mock and shock for some seems to be an end in itself rather than a necessary clearing away of obstructing cant and humbug so that there can be a resurgence of the creative human spirit.

The youthful reaction in Britain is still somewhat limited geographically, more associated with the big cities and the metropolis than with rural districts or market towns. Here, too, it has developed on much less exaggerated lines than in the U.S.A. There are not many traces in Britain of a typically 'Beat' influence. A few young 'weirds' do from time to time congregate in city cellars, or, astonishingly enough, at fashionable seaside resorts or in the grounds of some of the stately homes and country houses of the latterday aristocracy. But they are almost always no more than pseudo-beats intent upon self-dramatisation rather than total rejectors of the entire society who have nothing left to live for but the acceptance of their own nullity and the occasional neurotic kicks provided by drugs and forbidden eroticism. One reason for this is perhaps that post-war affluence in Britain was less marked and hence less disturbing. The crudity of North American prosperity probably required some institutional repudiation such as the 'Beats' provided—a total rejection of the 'American Dream' and denial of mass culture by a self-elected

1 Mary Morse in her book, *The Unattached*, Penguin Books, 1965, draws attention to the fact that many of the boys and girls outside formal youth groups had poor relations with their parents.

group of have-nots and impoverished romantics, many of whom, incidentally, are said to derive from comfortable middle class home backgrounds.

In Britain it is, or rather was, the 'Angry Young Man' and not the 'Rebel Without A Cause' who epitomised the more thoughtful type of young person's reaction against the mass of injustices and muddle which he has inherited from his elders.[1] It is the playwright, Arnold Wesker, or the poet, Christopher Logue here, and not, as we have already said, James Dean, who image youth's sharp rebellion against the regime of the 'old men', although there is some evidence of a drifting dissatisfied fringe group to be observed here and there. Theirs is an intellectual and aesthetic revolt, a striving for personal identity, the attempt to utter as a unique individual voice amid the babel of mass culture and dishonesty. Logue's period in prison, his career as a gun-runner and subsequent cashiering from the Army and his spell on National Assistance are the melodramatic episodes in an appealing career which are positively poetic, hence creative in character. The 'Angries' in England have fought a bitter war against the sham respectable façade that masks reality, while the 'Beatniks', on the other hand, seem to be set upon rejecting a way of life which appears to them to be totally corrupt and contemptible. The Angries are basically social reformers, not world-rejectors. Undoubtedly the 'Angry' movement here has been an intellectual and artistic renaissance more than any deep-seated wish to throw the whole of our society overboard.

There is a curious connecting thread between Beatnik society, teenage cults like that associated with the late James Dean, Angry Young Men, artistic Bohemians of the familiar kind, the tough teenage gangs and the pop stars' fan clubs. All seem to be to varying degrees manifestations of a similar rejection of the established way of life, the self-conscious assertion of youth as a self-justifying age-group and a strange mixture of reactive narcissism and nineteenth-century romanticism. To some extent these feelings have been synthetically produced and encouraged by profit-hungry commercial exploiters; to some degree they are the inevitable concomitant of early economic independence; and they also derive impetus from genuine sentiments of youthful idealism and traditional

[1] It is not often realised that the Angry Young Man phenomenon was not a new one and that it occurred after the First World War, too. See for example, Willie Maddison in Henry Williamson's novel sequence *The Flax of Dream*.

despair. Never before have so many of these interweaving strands been brought together, and it is this fact which gives contemporary youth culture both its compelling interest and social importance.

5

In this country as elsewhere in recent years a great deal of time and attention has been given to considering the problems of the 'unattached' who seem to have little aim or purpose in life.[1] They are to be found hanging around coffee bars either in 'swish' or 'sleazy' premises. Here, in a relaxed atmosphere, assisted by half-darkness and unending and often blaring background music, they can jive or rock or twist or shake according to the current craze to their hearts' content. 'Coffee-and-cuddles' does not, however, epitomise the nadir of moral depravity, although if it leads on to what is expressively known as 'heavy petting' it obviously may, by arousing strong physical passion, promote sexual experimentation of a not very desirable nature. But the life of the teenage hangouts is by no means all kisses in dark corners. A great deal of the time is spent on the floor, jiving or twisting, or just bunched in almost immovable clusters as the whole concourse slowly circulates to the sound of a beat group, in the corner, reflected off the low ceiling in a haze of mingled heat and body scents.

But patrons of the new and ever increasing coffee bars and similar teenage haunts are, more often than not, just ordinary young people having an evening out, enjoying the unconventional atmosphere and as aware as anyone of its essential unreality. In any university town undergraduates are found patronising such institutions, sitting and dancing alongside their more proletarian brethren and not necessarily doing themselves or their studies any great harm. The coffee bar is no more abominable a meeting place for the teenagers than the pub is for their parents. Indeed, in some ways it is clearly much less noxious.

Teenagers nowadays obviously enjoy massing together. They like being loosely associated in large bands. Over two and a half thousand will link up for a cross-channel fraternisation with their French coevals. Catered for by many bands and paying a fee of two guineas a head, they dance their way from Dover to Calais and back again for a weekend outing. All-night carnivals or unending dance sessions

---

[1] See especially in this connection, Mary Morse, op. cit.

attract them in vast numbers. Such gatherings can turn out to be harmless enough; equally they may end in trouble if the police get edgy and some group oversteps the narrow bounds of tolerated misbehaviour. In Southern Sweden, not long ago, over a thousand car-loads of youths descended on Karlskoga for the annual car races, ending up in a round of vandalism and similar orgies under the influence of drink. Girls stripped themselves naked, boys beat off police attempts to restore order and decency. A pitched battle ensued. It has happened there before and elsewhere in Sweden and the same sort of thing is reported in the United States and occasion-ally here.[1] Beaulieu jazz sessions have ended in 'bashings up' and teenage hysteria. But these things are still the exceptional not the normal way of behaving even for the more outlandish young people.

Of course there is a nihilistic element to be found by those who look for it. Sometimes groups of young people do break out in fits of apparently inexplicable and evilly intended violence. But, without in any way wishing to minimise the seriousness of such events, it must be said that these incidents are rare in Great Britain and that sometimes they can be actually provoked by injudicious police action.

Even undergraduate rags have in some university towns in recent years reached an unparalleled degree of rowdiness and violence. In some cases this has led to court proceedings, occasionally to students being sent down or rusticated, while some university authorities have also been obliged to ban public processions altogether in order to maintain civic order.

What may be called 'the climate of prevailing opinion' exerts a significant influence not only on traditional behaviour associated with rag days and mischief nights, but also on our methods of gauging the amount of delinquency committed. There is a general belief, expressed by most authorities on the subject, that young people in all European and American societies are more abandoned and delinquent in their behaviour than ever before. The rising tide of juvenile crime is noted with alarm in every western country and one writer, T. R. Fyvel, has gone so far as to speak of what he calls 'the Teddy Boy International' to describe the growing destructive element on the part of modern youth.

[1] The clash between the so-called 'Mods' and 'Rockers' which took place at Clacton in the Easter holiday of 1964 is a fairly mild example of the same kind of behaviour.

Fyvel ascribes this alleged rising crime and violence amongst young people and children to 'something in the way of life, in the break-up of traditional authority, in the values of the news in the headlines' encouraging 'widespread youthful cynicism in general and rather violent delinquency in particular'.[1]

It is, then, in the terms of this argument, a product of social change. It proceeds *pari passu* with a rising standard of living and, in a real sense, is the result of growing material affluence. The Teds, to use the older name, are the emotionally insecure members of this society, they are cut off from obtaining many of the desired rewards so conspicuously enjoyed by others and their bad behaviour is to be interpreted mainly as a protest against being the also-rans while, at the same time, affording them some kind of compensatory fantasy existence in which violence, nonconformity and general intransigence enable them to prove themselves and achieve their own somewhat warped kind of social status. It is a challenging and searching argument, closely in line with the more sociologically sophisticated theories of Albert Cohen and other American writers who have recently tried to analyse the basis of contemporary criminal subcultures.[2]

For Cohen, the delinquency of lower class boys is essentially a way of dealing with their problems of social adjustment, of achieving status by illicit means because it is denied to them by the law-abiding respectable society at large. Its hallmark is a repudiation of middle class standards and the deliberate adoption of their opposites. The delinquent subculture also legitimizes aggression which lower class youth are said to feel towards higher class people 'with their airs of superiority, disdain or condescension.'[3] Cohen is of course speaking specifically of American society and in so far as the basis of this is anchored in middle class values, aspirations and standards he finds 'the American way of life' a root cause of both subcultural crime and middle class conformity. 'The same value system, impinging upon children differently equipped to meet it, is instrumental in generating both delinquency and respectability.'

I am also inclined to think that there is something in the

1 T. R. Fyvel, *Troublemakers*; Schocken Books, 1962, p. 34.
2 Albert Cohen, *Delinquent Boys, the Culture of the Gang*; Routledge and Kegan Paul, 1956, and R. Cloward and L. Ohlin, *Delinquency and Opportunity*; Routledge and Kegan Paul, 1960.
3 Cohen, op. cit., p. 131.

reasonable, moreover, to accept it as a fact that not only
offences reported, but also that more are being committed

Drug addiction amongst teenagers is also much more cc
although compared with the United States the problem in i
is minimal and confined for the most part to a few of the
decadent and Bohemian parts of the larger cities, and in partic
London where, according to police allegations, cigarettes made fr
Indian hemp are sometimes sold at teenage parties for as much
six shillings each. There is also a small but vigorous black marke
supplying teenagers with 'purple heart' pep pills. Drunkenness is
also more widespread and apparently on the increase even amongst
girls. The number of prosecutions for being drunk and disorderly
for the 17–21 age group has never been so high as it is now. Moreover, crimes of violence amongst the same section of the population
have reached an all-time record.

It is as well to remember, however, that when we speak of the
delinquents or other youngsters giving trouble to their parents or to
society, we are still speaking of a small minority of those at risk.
No more than 2 or 3 per cent of the entire age group appear in court
on charges of serious (indictable) nature in any twelve month period.
The vast majority still manage to grow up and enter upon their
adult lives without undue difficulty. There is a real danger of the
entire juvenile and teenage group being stigmatised on account of
the problems presented by the minority. We do not want to exaggerate the proportions of the problems of childhood and youth in
contemporary society. Excessive concern could well induce fresh
anxiety which in its turn could lead to increased difficulties both for
youngsters and for their parents and mentors.

Even juvenile and adolescent gangs can appear more menacing
than they really are. As Peter Scott has said, generalising from his
experience in remand homes, clinics, clubs and other institutions
designed for the young, the adolescent street groups 'are not really
much concerned with delinquency' as a group, even though sometimes individual members may break the law.[1] 'In short,' he says,
'they look very fearsome, and maybe behave abominably, but they
are not often actually charged with offences.' Dr. Scott describes
these groups of boys and girls gathering at street corners, gossiping
at coffee bars or cafés and generally larking about together in their

[1] Peter Scott, 'Gangs and Delinquent Groups in London'; *British Journal of Delinquency* 7: pp. 8–21.

cial traditions of particular sorts of lower class society which are
ositively favourable to certain kinds of illegal behaviour. Rooming
house districts, in particular, with their confused standards and
shifting population, seem to be especially criminogenic. Moreover,
the traditional kind of long established slum where ganging is
endemic, where toughness is a highly prized value and where there
is often a restless search after something exciting to do, is also a
most powerful contributor to the growth of a delinquency-prone
culture pattern. Delinquency in these places is in the very air that
people breathe. It may owe something to a social protest against
past deprivation but in the here and now, it survives very much
under its own volition as an integral part of the pattern of everyday
life.[1]

6

The main grounds for the common assertion that young people
nowadays present grave social problems which as a community we
ought to be taking action to prevent comprise, amongst less serious
things, aggressiveness, drunkenness, drug addiction, criminality and
sexual promiscuity.[2]

Crime figures, incidentally for both adults and juveniles are everywhere considered to be on the increase. Juvenile crime in Britain,
that is to say reported crimes known by the police to have been committed by those over eight, but under seventeen years of age, have
about doubled what they were pre-1939. This is indeed the typical
situation throughout Western Europe. Even allowing for the bulge
in the post-war birth rate and the fact that the juvenile population,
especially of boys, has increased compared with 1938, there can be
little doubt that much more delinquency is *known* to be committed
by recent generations than by their parents and grandparents. It is

[1] Walter B. Miller has advanced a similar thesis in criticism of the point of
view put forward by Albert Cohen. See, for instance, 'Lower Class Culture as
a Generating Milieu of Gang Delinquency', *Journal of Social Issues*, Vol. 14
(1958), No. 3, pp. 5–19. David J. Bordua's paper, 'Delinquent Subcultures:
Sociological Interpretations of Gang Delinquency', *Annals* of the American
Academy of Political and Social Science, November 1961, *Teenage Culture*,
pp. 119–36, is a most interesting discussion of the whole topic.

[2] For a most interesting comparative examination of these criticisms see
Teddy Boys and Teddy Girls, International Child Welfare Review, Vol. XV,
No. 4, 1961, especially Dr G. Mik's article, 'The Psychological and Psychiatric
Aspects,' pp. 225 *et seq.*

off time as being mainly concerned in such antics with 'self-display and mutual support in the difficult business of extricating themselves from an uncomfortably close emotional dependence at home.' They are, hence, transitional groups designed to assist youngsters to get over an otherwise awkward stage of their development. 'When the home carapace is shed the group offers a shelter in which a new skin may harden—a breathing space for the acquisition of confidence.'[1] Although there may be occasional signs of regressive behaviour in these loosely structured groups of age-mates resulting in fighting or other misdemeanours, the majority may be described as 'quite innocuous, and, indeed, perhaps necessary and useful.'

The author adds: 'It is by no means always incumbent upon us to go out and work upon them or "socialize" them.'[2] Even though weapons may sometimes be carried by these groups' members, they are usually worn more for display purposes and as symbols of masculinity than kept in readiness for a 'carve up.' A gang in the true sense of the word following Frederic Thrasher's monumental investigations in Chicago over thirty years ago, must have an observable structure.[3] It has a leader, a closed membership, a regular meeting ground, some initiation rituals, a degree of continuity in time and definite delinquent purposes. Such gangs are remarkably few and far between in Britain, however widely they may be encountered in North American cities. 'It is indeed difficult,' Dr Scott writes, 'to find good examples of gangs, nor do the few that are found conform with the picture of healthy devilment, adventurousness, pride of leadership or loyal lieutenancy, that is often painted. Gang-members who come before the court usually have a gross anti-social character defect and come from homes in which the emotional atmosphere has been obviously disturbed and detrimental.'[4]

Such groups in Britain and other continental countries are mainly ephemeral in nature and comprise lonely, disturbed and often

---

[1] Peter Scott, 'Gangs and Delinquent Groups in London'; *British Journal of Delinquency* 7: pp. 8–21.

[2] Ibid.

[3] Frederic Thrasher, *The Gang*, University of Chicago Press, 1927.

[4] Peter Scott, op cit. A recent American study of teenage gangs in New York tends to confirm this diagnosis. See Lewis Yablonsky, *The Violent Gang*, Macmillan, 1962. Yablonsky suggests that the gangs are not nearly so large or so well organised as is often supposed, but consist in the main of a central core of near-psychopathic and sociopathic leaders surrounded by a largely illusory penumbra of subordinates and supporters.

pathetic characters, united in a sullen hostility to the police and
the outside world, but nourishing amongst themselves very little
abiding substitute satisfaction for what their lives have chronically
lacked in the past. They are much more of a social pest than a
menace. In a recent international report there were few indications
that widespread serious delinquent gangs existed outside America,
although the Polish report referred to such alarming symptoms as
'the so-called "gang-shag" ' as an outlet for collective sexuality
practised either upon 'a "baby doll" of the group' or even
occasionally on by-passers accosted in the street.[1]

But the delinquent gang proper has very little chance of surviving
with modern police methods. Hide-outs soon become spotted and
once the leaders have been prosecuted and institutionalised the group
is more likely than not to collapse and disintegrate. For the leaders
are the focus of the group's activities. It is they who set the pace and
drive their followers to greater and greater acts of daring and
delinquency. They are very often tense and strung up, with a permanent animosity towards the world, like Pinkie in Graham Greene's
novel, *Brighton Rock*, a classic example of the affectionless personality who had abandoned himself, despite his Catholic upbringing,
to a life of remorseless evildoing.

7

Many older people so dislike the ways in which some young people
dress and conduct themselves in public that they attribute all manner
of wickedness to them on the slimmest of evidence. The mere wearing
of tight jeans is taken as a self-evident sign of immorality. Any form
of narcissistic self-display is interpreted as morally wrong. Our
Victorian and Edwardian forebears, for all their pseudo-modesty
and prurient camouflage, were a good deal more lenient in this
matter than some people are today. If we were to go further back
in history, say to the sixteenth century, even greater flamboyance
amongst the upper class fashionable set would be found. The white
tights, puffy embroidered doublet, laundered ruff and profuse brown
curly hair of the elegant young courtier of those days were un-
compromisingly dedicated to what Herrick called 'cleanly-wanton-
nesse.' This may not be such a far cry from the high-school boys of
California who are said nowadays to peroxide their hair to make

[1] *Teddy Boys and Teddy Girls*, op. cit.

themselves more irresistible. The idea of trying to make oneself look as physically nice and attractive as possible may offend stubborn puritans, but it is not altogether inconceivable that beneath a charming exterior there may also be an honest heart and a keen mind. The Athenians who worshipped bodily perfection also reached an unequalled peak of intellectual and spiritual beauty.

All this is not to say that there are no signs of mass hysteria discernible in certain aspects of adolescent behaviour.[1] The wild, unrestrained adulation of pop singers (carefully nourished and contrived by their publicity managers and business promoters) is one glaring instance. Hordes of screaming teenagers mobbing stage doors, or rolling abandonedly in the theatre aisles, are not sights reassuring to one whose faith in human progress is already shaky on other grounds. There are also 'fan clubs', again promoted for reasons of financial exploitation by the amusement world harpies. These clubs swell like mushrooms almost overnight and traffic in autographed photos of the stars and similar idolatries.

There has undoubtedly been a striking change in the whole business of pin-up provision. In the past, since the consumers were usually males, the trade served up a series of gorgeous and scantily clad young maidens, snapped from any number of irresistible angles, to activate the masculine glands. Since those more male-dominated days, women have advanced further and further into the economic world, and their specific tastes have to be catered for in an appropriate way, from the muscular appeal of the latest Tarzan to the tight pants and leg-gestures of the newest pop singer rave. The new pin-up stereotype is no longer solely the show-girl or bathing belle, but more often than not an attractive proletarian male with a mournful face, wearing open-neck shirt and leather jacket, or even a plump young rock'n' roller in his pyjama bottoms or bathing trunks disporting on a Caribbean beach.

There is undeniably a great deal of adult stimulation behind the growing teenage cult. But it is also true to say, I think, that young people have responded with avidity to the opportunity thus afforded them to parade their differences and demonstrate their group solidarity in the face of a sometimes hostile and usually perturbed public opinion.

The teenage cult consists mainly in idealising and glamourising youth as opposed to maturity. Being young, in this context, is in

[1] The recent outbreak of 'Beatlemania' is a further example of this tendency.

itself supremely valuable. Nothing else is so precious as this perishable, fleeting youthfulness. After twenty-five, senescence begins and after that comes the long weary twilight of approaching death, which lasts for another forty years or more. There is an element of childish regression involved in the cult and its devotees. It is similar in many ways to the toddler's repudiation of parental support and authority during the nursery stage—a necessary though irritating phase which assists the human weaning process. The Young Ones form the desired group. All others are outsiders, enemies, detractors. Two concomitant influences seem to have brought this post-war phenomenon into prominence. First, there is the natural need for people to live their own lives and find their own feet in the world. There is nothing whatsoever new about this and nothing to be frightened about either. The second element is more sinister and involves the exploitation of young people's vulnerability for purely commercial ends.

We are all greatly indebted to Mark Abrams for the admirable way in which he has documented the rising affluence of youth in this country.[1] He has shown that, for the first time in British history, the adolescent age group has enough purchasing power to make it a worthwhile target for commercial exploitation. He has demonstrated that the 15–25 group, which in 1959 contained approximately five million unmarried youths, was in a position to spend some £830 millions a year—a modest sum perhaps by North American standards, but something altogether phenomenal in this country.[2] This was in addition, however, to £70 millions put on one side as savings, most of which, we should imagine, would be spent in the shops and stores in the not too remote future, or in providing continental holidays. While this does not comprise a very substantial proportion of the nation's consumer expenditure, it is nevertheless of great interest in so far as it corresponds to an entirely new source of purchasing power. Before 1939, when unemployment was rife and all too many youngsters languished in 'dead-end' jobs or were very poorly remunerated even in so-called steady and safe employment, there was no incentive for the commercial concerns to address their attention to children and young people. There was no youth market

[1] Mark Abrams, *The Teenage Consumer*; London Press Exchange Papers, July 1959 and January 1961.

[2] By 1965 it is estimated that there will be no less than 24 million teenagers in the U.S.A. with the sum of fourteen billion dollars a year to spend on themselves.

worth the name. But since the war, teenage incomes have risen very much faster than adults' and, in these terms, youth comprises the most affluent new section of the available market. There are, furthermore, some fields in which young people's custom is absolutely vital for continued prosperity. As the table reproduced below shows, there is a distinctive pattern of teenage 'spending for distinctive teenage ends in a distinctive teenage world.'[1] The clothing, cosmetics, soft drinks, cinema and gramophone record industries all rely heavily upon the juvenile customer. Comparative adolescent affluence has helped these trades either to maintain themselves or to become bouyantly expansive.

Mark Abrams calculated that the average male in the age group 15–25, who is unmarried, has, or had a year or two ago, about 71s. 6d. a week free spending money left over after meeting his basic commitments for board and lodging, while a female had rather less, about 54s. All this money, he claims, is spent on those goods and services which form what he calls 'the nexus of teenage gregariousness outside the home.'[2] With this means at their disposal they are able to enter into a symbiotic relationship with the commercial marketeers to create and enjoy the symbols of a characteristically adolescent culture. Particular songs and dance forms, even styles of dress and habits of life may be fairly innocuous and morally neutral. But it is also the case that young people are nowadays much more exposed to less desirable influences. Precocity of behaviour may arise to some extent from better nutrition and earlier physical maturation. It is also actively stimulated by advertising and the mass media. The advertisements of special brassieres for ten year old girls, which are printed in some periodicals, stimulate and express a desire to display 'glamour' and 'man-appeal' to a degree that we have a right to question. It is not that sexual interest is wrong or always to be discouraged. Nor is it to be accepted without demur that a generalised sexuality promoted by modern salesmanship is in society's or in the individual's best interests. It is not business and money making that is socially sacrosanct, but the human personality and the quality of corporate life.

There is little to be said in favour of the current techniques whereby sales promoters 'plug' certain styles and articles and so help to fixate adolescent tastes at an easily exploitable level. The plugging of particular song-hits and band numbers may not vitiate taste but

---

[1] Abrams, op. cit., p. 10. [2] Ibid.

merely favour some performers and discourage others. But when it comes to freezing life styles including speech, manners, customs and values, more serious social consequences arise. Reading books, being studious, even wearing glasses are all things which the admass world denigrates. Possessing personal glamour, sex appeal, alluring clothes and cosmetics and being in great demand with the opposite sex are things which these same advertisers identify with making a success of one's life. There is a danger that the profitability of the teenage cult may perpetuate the more lamentable features of juvenile culture. The fantasy of the new status group of 'Youth', idealisation of histrionic attitudes of extreme defiance or despair, may grow into an abiding social reality, permanently marking off young people from the rest of the community in undesirable ways. The institution-alisation of youthful alienation, once achieved, may prove extremely difficult to eradicate. In particular such more flagrant aspects of the revolt as promiscuous sexual experimentation possess obvious social dangers.

Until recently the British teenage market was almost exclusively working class, at least in taste and values. Since it was virtually non-existent before the second world war, the commercial promoters, as Abrams suggested, had no experience of the appropriate ways for creaming off adolescent affluence and had to turn to the United States for their models. It remains true, in the early nineteen-sixties, that proletarian styles and aesthetics predominate. Although Cliff Richard, for example, is the product of a grammar school education, his affinities as an artist are closer to the new working class values than to the traditional English bourgeoisie. I say new rather than traditional working class here because I believe that working class culture has recently undergone a change of emphasis. Without losing its essentially proletarian base it has incorporated some of the new forms of behaviour, especially expenditure on entertainment, holidays and personal appearance, which hitherto were economically out of reach. Instead of saying that many working class people have moved into the middle class and middle income sphere, I would prefer to say that they have created a new kind of culture, based on ideas of affluence, equality and personal pride, which are very foreign to the more humble and self-deprecating acceptance of inferior status which their grandparents practised.

The pop-singing idol to a considerable extent reflects this new proletarian image of the lower class youth who is transformed overnight into a successful variety artist. Tommy Steele, one of the older stars now moving rapidly away from the contemporary galaxy, was once a merchant seaman and lived with Mum and Dad in an ordinary Bermondsey street. Marty Wilde began cutting timber and Billy Fury was a deckhand on a Birkenhead ferry boat, while Cliff Richard worked for a time as an office clerk. Their later apotheosis is enhanced rather than diminished by such humble origins. Their achievement and those of many others indicates that there is now an alternative ladder to high status in our society which is completely free of ascriptive qualities and depends primarily on having skill, personality and the 'lucky break.' Athletics, and in particular professional football, opens up a similar prestigeful non-academic career to the boy from the ordinary background who has not passed any scholastic examinations. The images presented by these outstandingly successful 'golden boys' help to reassure their less conspicuous contemporaries that all is well with them and their group and that they need not feel ashamed either of lowly origin or of not having done well in school work. When a tousled-haired Cockney who has never made a film before, suddenly gains a £100,000 film contract, as Terence Stamp, ex-tugboat worker from Plaistow in the East End of London, did not long ago when he was given the title role in *Billy Budd*, all who are like him experience his success vicariously and are made to feel good.

The general tendency is almost certainly, as I have suggested, in the direction of the emergence of a new, more assured kind of working class culture.

The Edwardian costume, for instance, which used to epitomise a particularly defiant youthful intransigence, may have begun, as Fyvel[1] has argued in Savile Row and the West End, but quickly caught on in the East End which made this sartorial fashion its own. The new dandyism of the 'toughs,' however unattractive in its extreme forms, symbolised a new status and self-consciousness, and, in its turn, it gave an immense impetus to all kinds of experimental dressing on the part of adolescents everywhere. The roots of the change were international; their results were discernible across all class barriers. When Edwardianism melted into the more aesthetic-ally pleasing Italian styles, lower class youths still pioneered the way. Moreover, indications are not wanting to show that children of higher income groups are coming more and more under the sway

[1] Fyvel, op. cit., iv.

of the same general influences. For the first time, traditional bourgeois culture finds itself under strong pressure from what is a predominantly working class way of life. The cliché, 'we are all middle class nowadays', could be rephrased more accurately by saying that we are all constantly under both traditional middle class and rising working class influences. Boys and girls in grammar schools and universities, when given freedom of choice, favour the same kinds of distinctive clothes. Most young people visit soft-drink and coffee bars; many adore pop music and spend a lot of their free time drifting around doing nothing in particular with peer-group friends in very loosely knit gangs and clusters. It used to happen, of course, in earlier generations, but then there was much less provision for these teenage groups apart from the fish and chip shops.

One very interesting point to which Abrams[1] has drawn our attention is that there is now very little difference between the amounts of spending money at the disposal of working class and middle class boys. Spending by males accounts for no less than two-thirds of all teenage expenditure. The former have on average about 72 shillings and the latter rather less, about 70 shillings a week to disburse. A substantial gap, however, divides the two classes of girls. Girls from middle class homes have about 68 shillings a week available while their lower class counterparts have only 47 shillings. Thus in middle class culture boys and girls receive about the same amounts. But in the working class milieu the average young male has about twice as much to spend as the average girl, this in spite of the fact that females are obliged to lay out a good deal more than males on personal hygiene, especially on hair-do's and cosmetics. As far as the working class teenage market is concerned boys have a financial dominance which reflects the considerably higher wages they can earn soon after leaving school. It also suggests one of the reasons why, for lower class girls, marriage is still very attractive and one of the few ways open to them of improving their social and economic position.

As far as the pattern of expenditure goes, young people of all classes and both sexes showed a striking similarity. The bulk of the money seems to go on clothing and footwear, food, tobacco, trans-

[1] Abrams, op. cit., 1961 pamphlet, pp. 7–8. Although the actual wages of adolescents will have gone up since Dr Abrams did his enquiry it is not likely that the pattern either of earnings or expenditure will have changed very much.

	BOYS		GIRLS						
	Middle class	Working class	Middle class	Working class	All boys	All girls	All Middle class	All Working class	All teenagers
	s.	s.	s.	s.	s.	s.	s.	s.	s.
Food (including confectionery)	11·0	8·8	7·8	6·7	9·4	7·1	9·4	7·9	8·1
Drinks, soft and 'hard'	9·3	6·8	2·0	1·4	7·5	1·6	5·6	4·5	5·0
Cigarettes and tobacco	7·4	9·9	2·7	3·8	9·2	3·4	5·2	7·3	6·9
Clothing and footwear	8·3	7·2	24·9	14·6	7·8	18·0	16·6	10·4	12·3
Cosmetics, toilet preparations	0·4	0·9	3·0	2·5	0·8	2·7	1·7	1·7	1·7
Entertainment	5·3	5·5	2·3	2·5	5·4	2·4	3·8	4·3	4·2
Transport	8·7	6·1	9·0	5·5	6·8	6·7	8·8	5·8	6·8
All other goods and services	19·6	26·8	16·3	10·0	24·6	12·1	17·9	19·1	19·0
Total	70·0	72·0	68·0	47·0	71·5	54·0	69·0	61·0	64·0

WEEKLY TEENAGE EXPENDITURE BY CLASS AND SEX 1959
(in shillings)

port, drinks (soft and hard), and pure entertainment in that order. It certainly does not leave us with an impression of a rising generation which is either overwhelmingly reckless or utterly depraved. It does suggest, however, a group of people whose preoccupation is one or other form of self-indulgence and whose main responsibility is themselves. To say this is not to condemn them but rather to point out that they are very much in line with the general spirit of an age which emphasises the sensible policy of enjoyment to the limits of one's ability, an age of cruel paradoxes when welfare and comparative wellbeing have never been so widespread and the possibility of total annihilation so close. 'Enjoy yourself, it's later than you think' was the burden of a popular song some years ago and is still in tune with the times. Young people, perhaps, as always, seem to reflect such attitudes at their most logical extremes, but the philosophy is implicitly accepted in all age groups.

8

David Matza[1] holds that the three principal modes of youthful rebelliousness—delinquency, radicalism and Bohemianism—represent what he calls 'subterranean traditions' already existing within the framework of American society itself. These subterranean traditions link teenage intransigence to the traditions of the conventional community. Between the two apparently conflicting sets of values there exists this underground conversation, or, to use Matza's own words, 'there is an ongoing dialectic between conventional and deviant traditions and . . . in the process of exchange both are modified.'[2] The fact that this unseen correspondence continues suggests that conventional society is itself not by any means all that it represents itself to be. Not only do conventional versions of these deviant traditions exist in 'unalienated' sections of youth, such as in student society with its permitted radicalism and Bohemian eccentricities, but even amongst adult social groups there is a wide range of attitudes ranging from full acceptance and approval through to vicarious enjoyment from the touchline. This argument is very similar to the one that posits criminals as being socially necessary in order that we may, through contemplating them, relieve in fantasy our own forbidden and sinister desires.

1 David Matza, *Subterranean Traditions of Youth*, in *Annals* of the American Academy of Political and Social Science, November 1961, pp. 102–18.
2 Ibid.

Matza makes the interesting suggestion that the very existence of these conventionalised versions of subterranean deviant traditions assists young people to find their way back to a normal way of life when their rebellious stage comes to an end. These conventional versions of hidden deviance are, he argues, what we usually mean when we refer somewhat loosely to 'teenage culture.' Moreover, the very existence of the latter may itself help many youngsters to refrain from going too far in the way of outright deviancy. Teenage culture is thus seen as a fortuitous safeguard against delinquency and true rebellion. It may hence have a benign aspect. To quote Matza once again: 'although teenage culture may sometimes act as a preparation for the delinquent tradition, as its critics would have it, there seems little doubt that it often serves the functions of prevention and restoration.' At the Bohemian level we may also see a connection between authentic artistic rejection of the social order and the more 'bloody-minded' kind of intellectual student reactiveness. Thus, as the years of youthful dependency wane, the need to rebel automatically becomes less and less. Moreover, a proportion of the adult population are already sympathetically disposed towards adolescent intransigence and rebellion, so that the way to the re-integration of youth with normal society is already well prepared. Matza argues that the existence of conventional versions of the subterranean traditions is one further and very powerful factor assisting this necessary process.

9

Similar institutions have been created in most parts of the world to help to deal with the problems young people present to their elders. In England the Youth Service has developed since the passing of the 1944 Education Act as a part of the informal education of young people between the ages of fourteen and twenty. Its purpose has in general been to assist them to make a constructive use of their adolescent years. By and large, both the statutory and voluntary youth organisations have derived from middle class value systems. They arise in the main from a sense of unease on the part of the more successful members of society over the apparent aimlessness and aggressiveness of working class and lower income group youngsters. They have in a variety of ways provided the latter with harmless outlets for energies which might otherwise have been channelled into definitely anti-social acts. The Youth Service is an essentially bourgeois, and now an increasingly bureaucratic, attempt to palliate the social strains generated by class and status differences. It is usually conceived as something which the community as a whole undertakes for its young people, but, in fact, it is nearly always a service offered by the more to the less privileged. Its roots are deep in all that is best in Victorian philanthropy. One result of this rather moralistic bias in recent years has been the reaction of a small section of youth against this paternalistic attitude. A number of spontaneous youth groups have arisen, some very short lived, others of a more durable character, in which the leadership has entirely sprung from the body of the members and not been imposed from above.[1]

The self-programming club depicted perhaps a little too glamorously in the Cliff Richard film, *The Young Ones*, is a prototype of this kind of group that he himself once belonged to as an unknown singer. Such spontaneous groups represent an attempt on the part of self-conscious teenagers to run their own affairs without help or interference. They seem to meet specific teenage needs in ways which are satisfying to the customers rather than to the educationists and social workers who have hitherto monopolised the orthodox Youth Service. The promoters of these clubs which are run by teenagers strictly for teenagers, hang-outs of the young ones only, claim that they and they alone truly represent adolescent culture. One of the most publicised of these ventures is the one which Ray Gosling was associated with in Leicester.[2] Gosling claimed that 60 per cent of the young people eligible for the Youth Service were completely alienated from it and from what it stood for and offered. He advocated something much more like a students' union, a relatively rich set of miscellaneous 'organisations run by the students for the students.' However misinformed he might have been about the precise nature of undergraduate responsibility for the administration of its own recreative affairs, the point can, I think, be well taken, that for a long time youth, like the peoples of former colonial

[1] See *Spontaneous Youth Groups*, ed. by Peter Kuenstler, University of London Press, 1955.

[2] *Lady Albemarle's Boys*, A Young Fabian Pamphlet, Fabian Society, London, 1961.

territories, felt themselves to be over-organised, ultra-protected and seriously underrated. The time has come, in fact, for them to have greater autonomy, at least as far as leisure time activities are concerned. There is a dichotomy between 'those who connect' and 'those who care.' The former all too often connect in order to exploit youth commercially, while those who care can be hopelessly out of touch.

1

In English society maturity is achieved over a comparatively long period of time. It is not finally attained until legal majority commences at the twenty-first birthday. From that date onwards the individual is a full adult member of the community, enjoying the same rights and privileges and subject to the same laws and exposed to the same pressures and obligations as every other mature citizen, although even at this age he may not yet have achieved full economic independence. Up to that time, parental and pedagogical controls are gradually eased off in a series of haphazardly fixed stages, depending to some extent on social class position, on whether or not the individual is in receipt of full time education and, above all, on the ideas and theories of parents. The influence of friends, the pressure to conform to the local peer group culture and the strength and thrust of the individuals' own personalities all enter into the picture and add to the general confusion.

There is really no standard pattern or uniform maturational system in operation throughout the community.

The emotional instability and general turbulence which have long been associated with adolescence in our kind of society may very easily arise as a result of the indeterminate status of the adolescent rather than from innate constitutional causes. The so-called 'storminess' may be the outcome of social indeterminacy of role rather than inevitable psychological stress. This indeterminacy is amply illustrated in the various steps to maturity already referred to, the series of social bonuses grudgingly conceded, as a result of pressure, in a piecemeal and uncoordinated way, like rights of citizenship wrested from a tyrannical autocracy. A child is obliged to attend school in Britain until the end of the term in which he reaches his fifteenth birthday. Absenteeism can lead to prosecution in a juvenile court and committal to an approved school. He is subject to the juvenile court until he reaches the age of seventeen. Thereafter his offences are treated by the ordinary adult magistrates' courts, or, if of a much more serious nature, by a judge and jury at sessions or assizes. He may, after that age, be hanged if found guilty of homicide. At sixteen a youngster is permitted to leave home but is still subject to parental discipline in many ways. At this age a motor cycle—the most deadly weapon on the road—may be ridden though a licence to drive a car is withheld for a further twelve months. It is a criminal offence to have sexual relations with a girl under the age of sixteen. But a girl one day older than that age is considered differently and is deemed to have sufficient understanding of what is involved for any male who offends against her sexually to get off much more lightly. Nevertheless, no juvenile is allowed to marry before the age of twenty-one without parental consent. Boys, like their sisters, are still deprived of the vote until full legal majority is reached even though, until recently, they were considered to be mature enough for military service by the age of eighteen. A youngster cannot be served with alcohol in a pub under the age of eighteen nor with tobacco or cigarettes under the age of sixteen. If committed to the care of the local authority, under the Children and Young Persons Act, upon reaching their seventeenth birthday both sexes are immediately free to live their own lives without further supervision.

There is no doubt that this long drawn out period of social apprenticeship produces stresses and strains as a result of its anomalous nature. It is probably necessary, for many reasons, to have some transitional stage between childhood and maturity. It is probably true, too, as Dr Wall, for example, has pointed out, that this period nowadays needs to be a good deal longer than it used to be.[1] In the past there was much less to be learned before embarking on one's life's work, but this protracted waiting period is not necessarily a disadvantage. It may, if properly controlled, positively enrich both personal and social life. Says Dr Wall:

> Indeed it is not fanciful to attribute much of the flexibility and complexity of the modern personality, its cultural possibilities and its variety of adjustments, to the prolongation of adolescence which has come about in the last century and notably in the last fifty years. Not only is adolescence longer even for those who have always been favoured by circumstance; as a period interposed between more or less irresponsible childhood and full adult status, it has been extended to all classes and it is still, for a variety of reasons, growing longer.[2]

If one considers the status of the undergraduate, dependent on parental and public purse until after the age of twenty-one and

[1] W. D. Wall, *Child of our Times*; National Children's Home, Convocation Lecture, 1959, p. 57.
[2] Ibid.

possibly longer, it is apparent that something like a third of some people's effective life is passed in a kind of inferior apprentice position, denied full independence and complete autonomy. It is clearly something that weighs more heavily on the children of middle and upper class homes than it does on those who come from working class backgrounds. Thus it may be one strong reason why outlets for high spirits and ragging should be increasingly made available to those members of dependency groups who find their inferior status frustrating.

The point we have to grasp is that adolescence is both a psychological and sociological concept. Indeed, the social component is much more important than it used to be. In the past a lad went through a comparatively brief childhood and was more or less abruptly pitched into manhood. He began earning his living in the early post-pubertal stage and quickly assumed the airs and ways of the older folk. Nowadays, what the sociologists call the social roles are more complex and make greater demands on everyone. They take longer to learn, are exceedingly complex because of the growing technical complexity of our culture and require fulltime application. Moreover, increasing tenderness and sensitivity have led us to deprecate the abruptness with which, in the past, youngsters were expected to assume the adult role. We feel we ought to lead them more gently in the direction of responsibility, to let them have a longer time gradually accustoming themselves to the harsher realities of life. There is little likelihood, it seems to me, of our going back on these two important considerations. Both increasing tenderness and expanding technical complexity of work are here to stay.

One of the terms we have been using is 'role.' This is a concept which some sociologists use in describing the social structure. They think of society as comprising a number of functional roles, each with their associated statuses. The roles are filled by individuals. Each is more or less necessary for the achievement of social functions. As the latter change, so the roles may be expected to alter also. From the point of view of abstract analysis society is a very complex role system.[1]

---

[1] Sociologists distinguish between universal and particular roles. The former can be well illustrated by either a medical practitioner's more formal role *vis-à-vis* his patient or a lawyer's to his client. A particular role is more personalised. The relationships between friends or between kinsfolk are particular.

The roles in which the students of social structure are most interested are the instrumental ones closely linked to specific tasks which contribute to the continuity of the society as a stable and ongoing unitary whole. These roles are, of course, abstractions but nevertheless useful concepts that help us to think positively about what is going on in social processes and relationships.

The way in which an individual grows up socially and develops a social image, the manner in which he moves progressively through the various developmental stages in the direction of adult role playing, is of very great importance both to him and to the rest of us. The stability of the social role system depends to a considerable extent upon people learning to play their parts before the full and final drama of social life goes on stage. In his early years the individual is more concerned with enacting the more particular roles, roles which involve personal relationships and also those which are associated with special categories of people, e.g. infant, child, schoolboy, young person. It is often claimed by social psychologists that at this early developmental stage the child's capacity for understanding the nature of his role and his ability to carry it out successfully depend to a very considerable extent on the kind of emotional attachments he has with his parents and with other members of the family circle. Provided that adequate security and stability are maintained, the youngster is usually thought to be able to work his way progressively through the successive role stages of his life without undue deviation or difficulty. Psychologists stress the significance of the individual's relation to authority and authoritative figures in these early formative years. Those children who accept the authority of their parents and then the authority vested in teachers and other dominant representatives of the community, may be said to make a satisfactory and normal adjustment to the realities of their world. They learn first to obey and to respect authority, to keep the rules of adults and to toe the social line. But this authoritative relationship with parents or teachers cannot supply young people with another kind of social experience which is judged to be essential for the growth of the free democratic personality. The individual must somehow learn how to co-operate with others, more particularly how to live happily and work or play peaceably with his contemporaries and equals.

In the egalitarian relationship *vis-à-vis* his peers he can learn not only how to collaborate with others but also how to take responsibility for certain kinds of things.[1]

2

From what we have said in the preceding paragraph the crucial importance of the adolescent stage in the development of the truly socialised young citizen will be clear. The function of what we may call 'The Adolescent Society' is to enable the young person to become socially co-operative and responsible, precisely because these responses can only arise in a relationship of freedom and equality.[2] They cannot be expected to arise in the authoritative relationship between parent and child and between teacher and pupil.

Hence, youth is seen to be not only a logical but also a necessary stage in the socialisation process. The individual begins his adjustment and learning life as a child in what are sometimes called age-heterogeneous groups, largely composed of parents and kin. In these groups, the adults and particularly the parents are dominant. At a later stage, however, the youngster becomes associated with age-homogeneous groups. In the first place these are usually play groups and are encouraged by the dominant adults. Learning or school groups comes next and, as the individual grows older, groups of schoolfellows and personal friends selected by himself from amongst his contemporaries become more and more important.

In adolescence these age-homogeneous or peer groups are at the height of their influence. Sometimes, in fact, the adolescent seems to regard his or her contemporaries as the centre of the social universe, modelling behaviour on what the group approves and investing his entire emotional capital in his 'mates' or 'pals' or 'click' or whatever his particular set is called.

Association with age mates during the difficult transitional phase of youth is considered to be necessary for a youngster's mental health. Age mates have similar, sometimes identical, problems to face. Their needs, ambitions and anxieties mostly arise from the same sources. They grow out of problems associated with sexual maturation and the need to find a personal image and a social self.

[1] For a good description of the function of youth groups see S. N. Eisenstadt, *From Generation to Generation*; Routledge and Kegan Paul, 1956.
[2] Cf. Eisenstadt, op. cit.

Both the needs and the anxieties are, therefore, closely associated with the future roles that the youngsters will some day be called upon to play. Young people react at this stage in two main ways. In the first place, they are apt to be defensive and resistant towards the adult world. Their anxieties about whether or not they can ever perform the roles adequately make them want to avoid the issue, to turn back towards the comforting lesser responsibilities of childhood. Most adolescents regress to some extent during the teenage period. They have outbursts of boyish and coltish fecklessness and ebullient high spirits which sometimes get them into trouble with more uncompromising adult standards. But they are not merely apprehensive. They also experience moods of pleasurable anticipation, looking forward eagerly to the day when they will enjoy greater personal freedom and autonomy. Youth is, therefore, janus-headed, looking indeed a little wistfully back to childhood security, but also turning optimistically towards future responsibilities and adult rewards. Happily it is the latter mood which usually predominates and characterises the normal response.

In both reactions the peer group is reassuring. We can dream and plan the future with our contemporaries, we can also regress together and work out our anxieties as a group, cock a snook at the elderly and generally make a nuisance of ourselves. There is solidarity and companionship in the company of our fellows and equals, a warmth and romanticism which we have never experienced before and are not likely to again. Only in time of war do similar group feelings seem to be so splendidly roused and nourished.

Sociologists point out that, since individuals no longer spend their adult lives solely with their families of origin and kinsfolk, these constructive contacts with age-mates are in a real sense training grounds for future social relationships which more and more must come to take on diffuse and generalised characteristics. Peer groups are primary, in that they are based on face to face relations which can gradually begin to supplant relations with parents and other blood relatives. At this time 'the human image of a given age grade becomes an important symbol of collective identification.'[1]

The symbol, or, perhaps we should term it, the youth totem, may be, as suggested, the pin-up singer or teenage Beat Group to which fan clubs and similar forms of youthful mass hysteria are directed; at grammar and high school, the ideal of the all-round scholar-

[1] Eisenstadt, op. cit., p. 50.

athlete. All such identifications are expressions of youth's need to discover a personal meaning and self image.

Youth groups are limited to the transitional phase and die away once the individual has attained maturity and is better placed to achieve in ways appropriate to the more important adult world. Youth ideologies tend to glamorise the transitional phase, thus simultaneously reassuring and rewarding those who are painfully conscious of their indeterminate social position. The youth cultures thrown up by the youth ideologies are temporary substitutes for more mature and hence delayed satisfactions. Immediate gratification of desires and aspirations within the specific age group compensates young people to some extent for deferred rewards and inevitable deprivations. They can at least achieve high status within their own ranks. But it is important to note that, in modern societies, young people do not attain full status via their youth groups, only substitute or compensatory rewards of an interim kind.

Youth is a period of preparation, hence of potential stress. It seems little good denying this contingency which is a necessary product of adolescent status in our kind of society and civilisation. To be told that the Samoans or the Indian Bhils arrange things differently and with much less tension that we do is an intellectually interesting irrelevancy.[1]

Adolescence is certainly a period of stress and strain in our culture and as no one has seriously suggested altering the culture very drastically it is likely to remain so. We must accept its difficulties, with moderations of course, and try to find ways in which some of the more serious problems can be eased.

3

Stable attitudes are difficult to achieve at the adolescent stage because society only intermittently and in special cases gives much recognition to youth. When it does so, it is usually in the form of highly organised movements, invariably of a strongly patriotic and political nature, as in the Komsomols of Soviet Russia or the Israeli Kibbutz. Fascist youth organisations revealed all the most sinister aspects of this kind of national movement during the Nineteen-Thirties. In Western society today youth groups are not based to the

[1] See, for example, Prof. L. Carstairs' Reith Lectures, 1962, *This Island Now*; Hogarth Press, 1963.

same degree on strong community lines. A good deal of time and attention both in British and North American youth organisations is given to individual development and competitiveness. Moreover, both in Britain and the U.S.A., youth organisations, if associated too closely with any particular political party or programme, are looked upon with some degree of suspicion. We tend to believe that a rich variety of groups, each with their different ethos and activities, will prevent totalitarian influences gaining a foothold through youth as they did in Nazi Germany. But generally speaking, in Britain, youth groups have been associated with more juvenile and politically very innocuous activities. The games, sports and athletic interests which youngsters naturally enjoy and strive to excel in have often proved useful safeguards against a political and social maturing which might easily have proved embarrassing to the older and more powerful sections of the community. The denial of the right to cast a vote, moreover, until after the age of twenty-one has further tended to depress youthful aspirations to make a significant impression on national life. The substitute youthful outlets which have been permitted and encouraged by the older generation have all been exercised with a fairly tight, however benevolent, control. Both in our 'public' and grammar schools and in our *pukka* youth organisations, emphasis has been laid on appropriate activities and strong sanctions invoked when necessary against inappropriate, or, as some would call them, subversive activities. A senior boy, for example, was expelled from a well-known English grammar school not very long ago because he took part in a C.N.D. demonstration in his out-of-school time. Such dictatorial action not only undermines parental responsibility but tends to discourage other senior pupils from thinking themselves part and parcel of the real community. The very uniforms and badges that are so striking a feature of English education, particularly at secondary school level, are designed to mark youngsters off in a special category of their own.

Schools—the formal educational institutions which constitute nine-tenths of the total system—are charged with the task of perpetuating the social culture and handing on the general tradition to the rising generation. Hence it is the O.T.C. or Army Cadet Unit which receives approval, not the small coterie of free-thinking rebels with their perhaps naïve political ideas. It is the pupils who conform to the ethos dictated by the teachers and the community who prosper and win whatever accolades are going. There is an overwhelmingly powerful conservative bias in the entire educational system against which it is very hard indeed for the individual to fight. Yet fight some do. This is clearly demonstrated by the fact that so many of our modern labour and socialist leaders derived from grammar and even public school backgrounds.

There is clearly then enough elasticity in the system for a few choice minds to rebel successfully, to think their own thoughts and come to an independent conclusion. Our schools are not totalitarian institutions stamping every youngster into a predetermined ideological mould. But they are by nature and function conservative. The great educational problem which a parliamentary democracy like Britain has to solve is how to harmonise traditional and novel elements within the same school system. Tradition and change are two sides of the one coin. Tradition is not always good nor is it invariably wrong. There must be room for growth, for change, for progress and evolution, and, for this reason, there must always be an element of challenge permitted. At the same time stability must also be ensured. What we should aim to achieve is a tradition open to modification, a system which both encourages conservation and promotes changes. Democracy, to survive as a worth-while form of social organisation, must be alert to its deficiencies even as it is proud of, but not deluded by, its past achievements. There must always be room within our educational institutions for nonconformists and those who challenge the system thoughtfully and conscientiously.

4

This brings us to what I consider to be the most important aspect of the function of youth culture in society. The teenage period can be the time when growth is fostered and promoted, when criticism is undertaken and the seeds of the future society are lovingly and intelligently nurtured.

Youth is thus seen to be not merely an awkward phase during which youngsters learn to adjust themselves to the prevailing climate of ideas and values, but a vital growing point for the future. It is a time of opportunity not of dysfunctional discontinuity. Youth is not a stage to be deplored, as our Victorian ancestors believed, but a phase to be accepted for what it is and carefully fostered. If we accept the teenage period as falling roughly between the ages of fifteen and twenty-five, as Mark Abrams has suggested, then the proper function of youth becomes more and more clear. Adolescence, youth, the teenage phase—call it what we will—has an appropriate function in relation to the whole social process. The seeds of future social change are sown and nurtured during those years when young minds and hearts are still open to the influence of idealism, when dreams may gradually be transformed into developing realities so that, when the new generation emerges into the final world of adult responsibilities, there is a strong determination to achieve those high hopes of brotherly solicitude, equality and sensitive autonomy which are the truest legacy of education at its best.

What goes on in schools, colleges and universities, therefore, is of vital significance for us all. But, while it is clear that schools and colleges help to mould the world of at least a part of the adolescent population, it is equally clear that formal education is not universally influential and effective. There is, in fact, sometimes a clash between the culture of the formal institution and what, for lack of a better term, we may call 'teenage society.' Youth is not so much torn between Sir Charles Snow's two cultures of arts and science, as between a culture largely based on working class peer-group solidarity and the commercialised entertainment world, on the one hand, and the individualistic, middle class, high school, and university career system on the other. The two cultures and systems overlap and the cleavage may not prove to be irremediable. But they constitute, nevertheless, a real division and one which expanding educational provision is far from eliminating.

5

We might summarise the argument so far by saying that the social function of adolescence is to ensure both stability and change. Youth not only channels the main cultural stream, it also exerts a strong influence in the direction of social change. Put in these terms the role of the adolescent is crucial, even a little intimidating. It seems as far a cry from the limited objectives of the 'ton-up' boys as from the narrow preoccupations of college students intent on passing examinations and gaining certificates as though such things were ends in themselves.

Youth is, however, a time of supreme social opportunity, not only because young people possess considerable vitality but also because, in a measure, we can influence the direction in which changes will occur by influencing what they will experience at their most formative stage. We cannot dictate how they will react but we can precribe what they will experience and share their thoughts and feelings with them.

Wisely handled, youth will come to learn and to modify the traditional social roles. And they will do this, not by chance or happy accident, but as a result of choice arising from a soundly based moral education.

The youth phase is therefore a time of opportunity and potential growth both from the viewpoint of the individual and of the society as a whole. No society can afford to leave what happens during this stage to chance or to the influence of those whose sole interest consists in manipulating young people's instinctive responses for their own commercial gain. The exploitation of youth is not only an offence against the personalities of boys and girls themselves, it is also an assault on society. The risk of exploitation grows greater every day as the scope of mass media expands and ramifies. Powerful commercial interests, some of them centred outside this country, exist to sell whatever will be most immediately attractive and financially rewarding irrespective of the effects on cultural ideas and standards of conduct. Deviant young people tend to become mesmerised by these more insidious lures. They concentrate, to quote Eisenstadt once more, on an exaggeration of symbolic aspects of adult behaviour, such as spending money for its own sake, dressing up to attract attention, and sexual experimentation.[1]

This kind of youth culture, which is basically irresponsible and reactive against maturity, becomes a focus for all that is deviant, defiant and uncreatively disruptive. It is the Beatnik and the teddy boy substratum once again. It arises because the transmission of roles is not rigidly uniform or universally enforced.

Change and instability tend to go together. The changes are usually but not always desired, the instabilities and their consequences are more often deleterious. Role prescriptions in our kind of highly mobile and complex industrial society must necessarily be fairly loose and permissive, stressing the value of individual autonomy as much as conformity. The problem of how the two may perhaps be most successfully combined, is as we have said, an educational problem. It is also a moral problem, for the kind

[1] Eisenstadt, op. cit., p. 309.

of society we want to create and the basic personality type, to use the social scientist's jargon, we wish to foster cannot be decided upon grounds of mere economics or of short-term political strategy and similar expediencies.

Not many young people deviate, perhaps not enough care to question the established order and are constrained to think critically and constructively about what society ought to be like and how individual citizens ought to behave. There is a problem of over-conformity as well as a problem of deviation to contend with: there are social problems which arise from a new kind of social anarchy and nihilism and others which are the product of excessive rigidity.

6

From all we have said so far, it will be clear that youth is a stage of life which can be viewed from several different angles. It can be thought of, first of all, as nothing more than a chronological phase; that is to say, a certain number of years separating childhood from adulthood, to be got over as quickly and peacefully as possible. Such a view denies, however, the traditional romanticism of adolescence, the Romeo and Juliet springtime which great literature, and poetry in particular, has portrayed as something intrinsically magical and desirable, a kind of golden age to be savoured before the dull grey pall of workaday responsibilities descend upon us.

The dichotomy between the poetic and the chronological interpretations could hardly be more extreme. There is also a purely sentimental view-point which distils an atmosphere of lax permissiveness and is based on a philosophy, if such it can be called, of 'you're only young once!' The sentimentalist retards youth while the moralistic inculcator tends to over-direct and inhibit. The sociological view is rather more sophisticated. While it should not dispel the idea that youth is a time for pleasure and enjoyment it also maintains that it is a necessary stage for the perpetuation of the traditional culture and as a lever for forcing changes in the structure of society. Such a view is dignified and challenging. The transitional peer group relationship, hence, exists in its own right. It is legitimated by important social needs. It bridges the past and the present and, at the same time, helps to mould the future.

A comprehensive concept of adolescence will be simultaneously sociological, psychological and moral. It will deal with individual

and social needs in their proper proportions. It will make allowance
for the dynamic of future development and social change as well as
for personal motivation and individual choice. This can best be
thought of analytically as comprising a series of tasks which have
to be undertaken in an unfolding process of personal and social
maturation. Young people, as it were, are all set a number of problems which they have to solve over a flexible number of years. It
is a kind of social intelligence test set for each individual in the most
concrete and practical terms. Some will solve these problems more
quickly and more efficiently than others. Some, indeed, may never
succeed in solving all the problems that life sets them.

These problems and tasks, which we all have to face and for which,
in the end, some kind of solution must be found, may be thought of
in both personal and social terms. We all have to solve the same
problems, although there will be differences of degree which will
distinguish individuals from each other and social classes from social
classes. The problems are set for us by the society and community
into which we are born. They are basic to our humanity and are
also deeply influenced by the climate of the social setting in which
we operate.

Because they are both personal and hence to some degree flexible,
and social and hence to some degree predetermined, these tasks or
problems are not easy to bring neatly within the compass of formal
legislation. This is one of the reasons why the discrepancies mentioned earlier occur,[1] and why maturity cannot readily be ascribed
merely by virtue of an individual's chronological age. Some will
mature long before the legal date is attained; others will drag un-
solved problems with them long after the age of formal adulthood
has been passed.

The nature of the tasks that have to be undertaken by the developing individual living in a modern society has been valuably outlined
by Havighurst in his *Human Development and Education*.[2] He
describes a 'developmental task' as one which arises at or about a
certain period in the life of the individual, successful achievement of
which leads to his happiness and success with later tasks, while
failure leads to personal unhappiness, social disapproval and
increased difficulty with tasks which lie ahead.

---

[1] See pp. 42–43.
[2] R. J. Havighurst, *Human Development and Education*; Longmans, 1953, and
David McKay Co., Inc.

The tasks are, therefore, closely related to each other, and failure at one level will almost certainly mean stress and strain at another level. The boy or girl who succeeds with the earlier problems is more likely to succeed with the later ones. In maturation, as in so many other aspects of life, nothing succeeds like success, and fortune favours the lucky.

Havighurst lists no less than ten developmental tasks which every adolescent has to undertake.[1] They are:

1. Achieving new and more mature relationships with age-mates of both sexes.
2. Achieving a masculine or feminine social role.
3. Accepting one's physique and using the body effectively.
4. Achieving emotional independence of parents and other adults.
5. Achieving assurance of economic independence.
6. Selecting and preparing for an occupation.
7. Preparing for marriage and family life.
8. Developing intellectual skills and concepts necessary for civic competence.
9. Desiring and achieving socially responsible behaviour.
10. Acquiring a set of values and an ethical system as a guide to behaviour.

Dr W. D. Wall, in his most thoughtful study, *Child of Our Times*,[2] suggests four main goals to be achieved between the ages of 13 and 25 which are in substantial agreement with those put forward by Havighurst. Dr Wall's points are:

1. A social self, 'oriented to others, aware of a place in society, of duties as well as privileges, and in general emancipated from egocentric dependence on parents or indeed on others.'
2. A sexual self, 'capable of a range of feeling from friendly indifference to deep involvement with a member of the opposite sex, adequate adjustment in marriage and the ability to found and care for a family.'
3. A working self, 'essential not only to economic independence but as a basis of self-respect and self-knowledge.'
4. 'An interpretation of life, philosophical, religious, political, vaguely or clearly formulated, something by reference to which major decisions can be taken and the behaviour and attitudes of others understood.'[3]

The goal may be thought of in terms of what has been called 'general adult competence' in relation to the norms of the wider

[1] R. J. Havighurst, *Human Development and Education*; Longmans, 1953, pp. 111–58.
[2] Wall, op. cit.   [3] Ibid., p. 77.

society and of the local community in which people happen to live. This may be analysed further, in orthodox social groups, into doing well at work (getting on in the firm or career and earning a rising income); succeeding in sexual and family life (getting married, having children); and being a useful citizen (law-abiding, responsible, sharing in public affairs and events). Less orthodox circles, either of Bohemian or other subcultural character, might well omit the third consideration of 'good citizenship': some might even regard economic success as distasteful, while others might well prize sexuality highly but deny the importance of either marriage or family life. We may safely assume that the norms of our society are closer to the norms of middle class culture than to those of any other subgroup and that the most powerful wielders of influence (moral and educational) are still those people who would, by and large, subscribe to the values of sound family life, conscientious work and responsible citizenship.

7

We frequently talk nowadays, following Jung, of the self-image. We emphasise the importance in the growing-up process of acquiring a sound and satisfactory concept of oneself, adequate both for one's inner personal needs and appropriate for the social environment. Jung calls this process, whereby a satisfying realisation of the self is achieved, 'the way of individuation.' Individuation means: 'Becoming an individual being, and, in so far as we understand by individuality our innermost, final, incomparable uniqueness, becoming *one's own Self*.'[1] This does not mean egocentricity but self-realisation within the surrounding universe. It is both individual and collective, personal and social, philosophical and purposive. Jung believed that one of the commonest sources of psychic disturbance in contemporary society arose specifically from a lack of meaning and purpose in life, a loss of faith in God and the decay of religious belief leaving nothing else to fill the spiritual vacuum. The mentally sick individual is the man who has lost the key to the meaning of his life and of the universe; conversely, the sane man is the one who has found his soul—the fundamental truth and light of nature which inheres to meet our deepest needs and desires.

1 From *Two Essays on Analytical Psychology*, quoted by John Jacob in *The Psychology of C. G. Jung*; Kegan Paul, Trench, Trubner, 1942, p. 100.

The problem facing the growing youth is how to make sense of self, of society and of the universe. Romantic youth is obsessed with egotism, totalitarian youth enslaved by the state, religious youth perhaps excessively devoted to other-worldly things and hence socially ineffectual.

We might usefully, therefore, put forward a developmental programme very similar to those supplied by Havighurst and Wall. It would involve:

1. Coming to terms with society.
2. Coming to terms with the self.
3. Coming to terms with life as a whole.

Coming to terms with society can be discussed under such headings as: being educated and getting a job, taking part in political and trade union affairs, bringing up children and so on. Coming to terms with one's self can be examined in terms of sexual relationships, developing one's talents in every direction, while coming to terms with life as a whole refers to the acquisition of a moral code and of more general religious beliefs.

These three are, of course, all dimensions of what is essentially the same process. The whole, healthy, fully integrated person has to achieve meaning and purpose at all three levels of being before a state of harmony may be said to exist in his personality. He will be dynamic yet at peace within himself. The full significance of self will be attained through sound personal relationships with other human beings and with the source and origin of life itself.

These are indeed the fundamental issues of humanity for all epochs. But adolescence is the time when they first flood upon us with compelling force and deep emotional intensity. Not for nothing has adolescence been singled out as the time of religious, spiritual and artistic flowering. It is the moment when awareness of self and other selves seems sharpest, when the essential loneliness of the individual is suffered most keenly, when we are most free from other commitments and responsibilities to concentrate on the great issues of life and death, love and rejection, faith and despair.

James Hemming[1] has demonstrated the tremendous need that young people have at this stage of their development for someone in whom to confide and discuss their problems with in privacy. His examination of the contents of many hundreds of letters sent by

[1] James Hemming, *Problems of Adolescent Girls*; Heinemann, 1960.

girl teenagers to the advice section of a weekly magazine has dram
atically revealed the gnawing sense of imperfection which youngster
experience at this time of life together with their most earnest desir
to grow into acceptable people. The demand for guidance in persona
problems is widespread.[1] Young people seem to experience the onse
of maturity as an overwhelming event. They seem, moreover, fo
the most part, to be left to find out their own salvation. Little help
guidance, support, comfort can be available for those thousands o
teenagers who write off their pathetic enquiry letters to the unknow
advisors in far away London week after week, year after year.

As Hemming says, 'what adolescents seek to gain through writin
to a paper should be available to them in personal relationship.'
But obviously for a great many young people today this help is no
forthcoming either from parents, relatives, teachers or friends, an
they are obliged to rely upon external guidance or to go without hel
altogether. The letters Hemming quotes are indeed a severe com
mentary on the failure of family and school to meet young people'
needs in a realistic and sympathetic way. They indicate, once agair
the isolation of youth in contemporary society and the gulf dividin
the generations.

1 Mary Morse, op. cit., draws attention also to the essential loneliness o
adolescence and stresses the need for the presence in their lives of sympathet
adults.
2 Hemming, op. cit., p. 36.

Part Two

1

Adolescence is generally recognised to be a period when the individual is simultaneously presented with growing inner and external demands. Unfolding emotional needs are accompanied by greater social pressures to conform and to find an approved social role. It corresponds to what Dr Wall has tellingly called 'not a bourne which a brief initiation ceremony overleaps but a no-man's land of six or more years.'[1]

The adolescent is constantly being compelled to come to terms with himself and with society. It is, therefore, misleading to separate these two fundamental aspects of development in any description of the maturation process. The self is always shaped by and adapted to the moulding matrix of the social environment. Instinctual drives and inherited tendencies are either facilitated or obstructed by the setting in which the individual is obliged to grow up. At the same time conscious efforts are directed towards tailoring the environment to some extent to meet the individual's basic biological and psychological needs. There is a kind of give and take between the human organism and the compulsions of the social structure so that we usually find various facilitative devices accompanying any inhibiting situation, and frustrations are, to some degree, compensated for by the provision of social palliatives, just as dock is often found growing alongside nettles on waste land. The formal Youth Service is one example of a facilitative and compensatory organisation created to meet the needs of young people at a particular stage of their development.

It is necessary to emphasise that growth takes place simultaneously but not necessarily harmoniously, along several lines. Nevertheless, since we cannot deal with every aspect at one and the same time, it is useful to divide the problems to be solved into those which are mainly personal and those which are more obviously social in origin. In this section we will try to deal with the latter, leaving the former to two succeeding chapters. This is a matter of analytical convenience rather than of choice. Quite obviously emotional and personal

[1] W. D. Wall, *Education and Mental Health*; UNESCO/Harrap, 1955, p. 136.

problems influence the way in which the individual relates to his fellows in society, impinges on his work in school or factory and deeply colours his philosophy of life. There will inevitably, then, be a fair amount of overlapping between the three chapters in this section of the book.

Perhaps the most useful way to deal with the business of how the individual comes to terms with his society is to divide what we have to say into two main parts: educational, and with a brief look at employment, political affiliations. They are all closely related. Obviously the kind of education boys or girls receive determines to a considerable extent the sort of job or career they take up later in life, and this, in turn, settles social status and, in theory at least, decides which political party is truly representative of their individual and occupational interests. There is, of course, no neat correspondence between social status and political sympathies and affiliation, though there is a very clearly observable connection between education and career.[1]

The central theme of this chapter may be called the problem of, or the problems associated with, social apprenticeship. They begin at home and in the classroom and continue into the workplace and polling booth. Home, school and work, the title incidentally of a valuable study of young people in the Sheffield area,[2] seem to be linked together as the main focal points of influence and effort which determine to a considerable extent whether or not a youngster 'gets off to a good start' in life and has a reasonable prospect of future success.

The subject is gigantic and one that can only be sketchily touched on in a study of this length. Here we can do no more than tease out the main threads and expose them briefly to view. This necessitates a quick glance at the social structure as a whole. Clearly we cannot hope to understand how the scholastic system operates or the kinds of jobs available unless we know how the community is divided and what kinds of educational institutions exist to help particular social groups and what the consequences of differential opportunities and expectations are for that age group concerned. At the risk of naïve

[1] See for example Olive Banks, *Parity and Prestige in English Secondary Education*; Routledge and Kegan Paul, 1955: Floud, Halsey and Martin, *Social Class and Educational Opportunity*; Heinemann, 1956: *Early Leaving*, A Report of the Central Advisory Council for Education (England), H.M.S.O., 1954; and David Glass, *et al.*, *Social Mobility in Britain*; Routledge and Kegan Paul, 1954.

[2] M. P. Carter, *Home, School and Work*; Pergamon Press, 1962.

over-simplification, I would suggest that one of the most important things about our kind of society is that it is extremely confused both about its social objectives and the various methods to be utilised. It is a society which demonstrably evolved from an aristocratic non-equalitarian order into which the notions of equality, of democratic freedom, only gradually percolated and slowly transformed men's thinking. The process is far from being completed yet, and it would be fair to describe Britain as a society still only moving in the direction of full equality and towards the realisation of what is involved in the word 'community.' Sectional interests everywhere prevail. Social class distinctions and stratification are amongst the more obvious social phenomena which, though taken very much for granted, strike the critical foreign visitor as deep-rooted and severe. The economic problem that faces us is how to ensure 'fair shares for all.' At the level of industrial discipline this involves getting everyone to do a fair day's work for an agreed and just reward. In most situations, it is unquestionably assumed that a man has a right to earn as much as he legitimately can command from his fellows, that private enterprise and personal initiatives are right and proper and should earn rich rewards and dividends. We accept the idea, moreover, of property and privilege being handed down from father to son. We believe that a man is free to 'do the best for himself' and that every parent ought to try 'to do the best for his children.' But getting off to a good start in life means in a free enterprise, capitalistic, market-regulated economy that others will inevitably be handicapped. It encourages 'oneupmanship.' It fosters privilege. It nourishes competition and breeds conflict as well as co-operation. Perhaps the major educational lesson to be learned by the young person is how 'to maintain both competition and co-operation in a delicate balance of forces'[1] necessary for success in modern urban societies. The child must learn how 'to compete but he must not *seem* competitive.'[2] The prevailing culture (especially of North America) presents the educationalist with an acute paradox which is never in fact satisfactorily resolved. Family life is based on values of companionship and emotional solidarity. So, too, is the friendship group and the clique of age-mates. But work and play are both competitive. So the culture prescribes, and the schools are obliged in their turn to create an educational environment which

[1] Seeley, *et al.*, *Crestwood Heights*; Constable, 1956, p. 229.
[2] Ibid.

fits in with this controlled competitive system. Boys fight to get int
the team; then they strive concertedly against other teams. Eac
tries his best to be selected and every team wants to win. High statu
well-paid jobs go to the hard workers, the lucky ones, the men wit
the requisite qualifications and to those with inside influence. Th
best, the luckiest, the ablest, the most influential men win.

Such is the ethos of what we sometimes term 'the world.' Th
world, in this sense, is opposed to the realm of spiritual valu
derived in the main from philosophical ideas about the intrins
worth of the individual, brotherly love and the vanity of earth
goods. The broad ethical values of Christianity, above all the u
comfortable injunction to love one's neighbour as oneself, are n
those of business and commerce and even less those of internation.
relations and politics. The religious truths taught in church an
chapel and even in religious instruction lessons demand the creatio
of a very different social order from that which exists.[1] A seriou
ideological tension arises which generates considerable strain fo
the children of 'believers,' and, as Seeley has pointed out, psycho
logical adjustment to this tension is far from being a cost-fre
business.[2]

In a social system based on private property, which encourage
competition and thrives on free enterprise, which is, moreove
deeply divided into various occupational and status groups or soci
classes, it is clear that some children are privileged and others ar
by comparison socially and educationally handicapped.[3] There
more than one educational system: there are in fact two, one privat
and the other statutory which, in the main, cater for distinctl
different income groups. All too often, these obvious facts are ne
discussed in books written for the benefit of teachers, educationa
psychologists or social workers. It is too often blandly assumed tha
all that determines the outcome of the educational process is th
skill of the teachers and the innate intellectual endowment of th
pupils, after some due allowance has been made for physical hand
caps. It is only in comparatively recent years that research has bee
concentrated on the sociological factors influencing academi
performance, and, in the first place, determining whether or not

[1] Seeley, et al., Crestwood Heights, Constable, 1956, p. 401.
[2] Ibid.
[3] Cf. J. B. Mays, Education and the Urban Child, Liverpool University Press
1962.

child gains access to the kind of school best fitted to develop his abilities and facilitate admission to a professional career. If 'other things' were equal, then knowledge of a child's I.Q., his aptitudes and emotional make-up would presumably enable us to help him select the most suitable school and the most appropriate and rewarding career. But these 'other things' never are in fact equal. Inequalities rule the day. Some families wield considerable influence and can pull a variety of strings to obtain the kind of education they desire for their children. A company director who is himself an old Cambridge blue finds it fairly easy to get his son a place in an Oxbridge college, provided, of course, the boy has ability. So son follows in the footsteps of father, wins his blue and makes some useful friends in the process, and eventually comes down with a decent degree to find the world more or less at his feet. A career in business, commerce, industry or the civil service, can be had more or less for the asking. Indeed, these days, representatives from the commercial firms land up on the doorsteps, or, rather, in the gateways, of Oxbridge colleges more or less touting for recruits.

The son of the docker, born in a back street, inherits an entirely different kind of world. If he has ability, works hard and is sufficiently motivated, he too can hack and hew his way through to a university education, and armed with colours and academic credentials make a good living for himself and his children. But such successes are all too rare. The old neighbourhood deadens and drags down the aspirant. He finds himself a social isolate. He is going in a different direction from his former mates and is estranged from the people of the district and even, perhaps, something of an outcast in his own home and family circle. The kin-group may be proud of his achievements but sometimes resent his ambitions to the point of virtual exclusion. The road to ultimate success for such a boy will be hard and long and often bitterly contended. There will be many moments of despair when he will want to abandon the course he has set out upon to return to the warmth and reassurance of the people he sprang from and feels he is leaving in the lurch. The saga of the modern 'scholarship' type has often been told and need not be repeated here. It is the tale of clashing cultures, of class barriers and social alienation and reveals in vivid detail the emotional price exacted from all who would climb the ladder of success.

It is necessary to keep these pictures in mind when considering school performance and the choice of career. On one side is the

gifted boy of the gifted, influential, wealthy father, getting off to a
flying start in life and faced on the threshold of manhood by an
exciting choice of more or less equally rewarding high status jobs.
On the other is the able boy of socially uninfluential parents slogging
every inch of the way through grammar school and finally university
until, in the end, in spite of misunderstanding, criticism and isolation,
he stands more or less shoulder to shoulder with his more privileged
counterpart. But between these peaks lie deep and thickly populated
dead-level valleys of non-achievement. The odds are always against
the children from lower class and always in favour of those from
higher class homes. As Jackson and Marsden have well argued:

Selection is not an event that happens and ends suddenly at 11 plus.
It is a process that is at work all the time from the moment the child
enters school to his final leaving: a gentle shaking of the sieve, with now
and again one or two big jerks.[1]

It is a fact, as the Crowther Report hammered home to us, that
nearly half the pupils with I.Q.s over 120 leave school at the age of
fifteen, and the great majority of these able 'early leavers' come from
lower working class backgrounds.[2] The entire culture of the lower
working class neighbourhood is against successful academic performance. Not only are the houses overcrowded, the streets over-
populated, the local primary schools understaffed and inadequately
equipped, but there has recently been shown to be a basic difference
in the actual language employed by the different social status groups.[3]

Basil Bernstein points to a fundamental restriction of vocabulary
amongst working class families which tends to produce low scores
in intelligence as well as in performance tests. What he calls the
'public' language of the working class area is apt to be over-des-
criptive and traditional, a kind of social shorthand for getting
through the everyday affairs of life but ill suited to abstract generalisations and the use of the kinds of concepts used by science and
higher learning. Middle class speech or 'formal' language, on the
other hand, is said to encourage the use of ideas and terms conducive
to academic study. The theory is interesting, though not entirely

[1] B. Jackson and D. Marsden, *Education and the Working Class*; Routledge
and Kegan Paul, 1962, p. 210.

[2] *15 to 18*, Report of the Central Advisory Council for Education (England),
H.M.S.O., 1959, p. 118, etc.

[3] Basil Bernstein, 'Language and Social Class', *British Journal of Sociology*,
vol. ix, no. 3, 1960, also 'Social Structure, Language and Learning' in *Educational
Research*, vol. iii, no. 3, 1961.

conclusive. It does, however, pinpoint the fact that there are deep cultural cleavages between the various income, occupational and status groups which constitute contemporary society. An extensive vocabulary, acquired at an early age, and an ability to think and talk in theoretical terms is undoubtedly an enormous advantage at school and university and children who are thus deprived are greatly handicapped in open competition with those who have enjoyed such training. All this boils down to the fact that education (in the modern sense 'schooling') is by and large a middle class invention and activity. The middle classes not only more or less invented secondary education in the form of the grammar school archetype but they have successively monopolised it ever since. Thus, as Jackson and Marsden have somewhat depressingly shown, those boys and girls from working class homes who do well at grammar schools and universities tend to be completely assimilated into middle class culture.[1] Those who have ascended the social scale via the educational ladder are seldom energetic on behalf of the less fortunate members of the group they have left behind them. Once they become established in secure jobs they seem to forget their own humbler origins and to be more bourgeois even than the established bourgeoisie itself. The most depressing outcome of Jackson and Marsden's study of the unvaliant 88 is the final picture of them at the end of the process, 'often rigidly orthodox citizens, who wish to preserve a hierarchical society and all its institutions as they now stand', and adopting, moreover, an often censorious and superior attitude to the lower class culture they have outgrown and to the 'dim ones' who did not gain a place at the local grammar school.

2

We may take it for granted that how a boy comes to terms with his society, how he is prepared for and ultimately obtains his job, is largely conditioned by his educational history, which is, in turn, substantially affected by the income and status of his parents. Family background does not absolutely dictate what kind of educational career a child obtains but it is undoubtedly a powerful determinant. Hollingshead decided on the basis of his Elmtown study that not only does the home affect a youngster's performance at school but it also influences his job aspirations and expectations:

[1] Jackson and Marsden, op. cit., passim.

'the jobs the adolescents have and their ideas about desirable jobs reflect significantly their family's position in the class structure.'[1] Rigidities in the social structure, above all in the educational system, and subcultural conflicts and discontinuities between the various social strata are exceedingly difficult to eliminate. As Friedenberg complained, 'The most tragic thing that happens to lower-status youngsters in school is that they learn to accept the prevailing judgment of their worth. They accept and internalize the social verdict on themselves . . .', and for such a pupil 'the school is merely the latest in a series of social institutions—beginning with his home —that have transmitted to him the same appraisal of himself. This, after all, is what social status means.'[2]

The 1944 Education Act intended to do away with inequalities and to enable a child's career to be based solely upon his age, aptitude, and ability, but it is demonstrably clear that this ideal of equal opportunity for all has not been realised and probably never will be until certain structural changes in English society itself are effected. The work of sociologists and psychologists in recent years has done much to prepare the ground for educational change by demonstrating the extent of wastage in the present arrangements and by undermining some of the hoary myths which have in the past been used to justify an unequal and inefficient system. One of these myths, that all the gifted pupils went on to selective secondary schools and did well there, has been trounced by various Ministry of Education reports and sociological enquiries. A second and much more venerable myth, that those who do not get places in grammar or technical schools are necessarily in some ways less able than those of their contemporaries who do, has also been demolished. But the idea dies hard that low intelligence is not a necessary cause of poor or indifferent academic performance. Teachers, especially, have clung obstinately to the idea that the tests they carry out purporting to ascertain the I.Q.s of their pupils are infallible indices of children's innate abilities and not merely very accurate prognostic devices to discover which boys and girls are likely to do well in secondary schools and which are not so likely.

Dr Agnes Crawford who undertook an enquiry into the reading ability and intelligence of a sample of school children in the Liverpool

1 A. B. Hollingshead, *Elmtown's Youth*; Science Editions, New York, p. 441.
2 Edgar Z. Friedenberg, *The Vanishing Adolescent*; Dell Books, Laurel Edition, 1962, p. 117.

area showed, to my mind convincingly, that we cannot take the teachers' findings for established and immutable facts.[1] When she, personally, and assisted by a group of teachers specially trained in the administration of psychological tests, examined a cross section of children at city primary schools it was found that there was very little difference in the performance of those who attended the poorer and older schools in comparison with those who went to schools in the better class districts. Yet the children at the latter schools did infinitely better at the General Entrance or as it is more commonly known the 11 plus examinations. There seemed to be no alternative explanation to account for these remarkable differential achievements other than to attribute them to existing social inequalities. Clearly the children in the neighbourhoods which did badly academically suffered from a cultural impoverishment, a general absence of parental support and consequent lack of motivation towards high achievement in school. It is also equally clear that the schools they attended, the teachers they met there and the widespread acceptance of the idea that they were not in any way being groomed for grammar school entrance contributed further debilitating influences which, in combination with the shortcomings of the local milieu and absence of parental stimulation, tended to create and to perpetuate a tradition of inertia and a pattern of typical underprivilege. The pupils in these down town schools were, on the whole, being prepared for second- or even for third-class citizenship, while, in sharp contrast, those in the comfortably off suburbs, deriving from families with traditions of grammar school education and of professional employment, were constantly being stimulated to emulate their parents and motivated to do well at school and university.

The importance of the educational system for future social structure can hardly be exaggerated. Sociologists have shown, beyond reasonable doubt, that the tendency for educational performance leading to the acquisition of paper qualifications is becoming increasingly important in determining the life style and prospects of the vast majority of the people of this country.[2] More and more, as the years go by, is it becoming important to have passed the right examinations, to have the right degrees or diplomas and to have been to the right schools and universities. Less and less

---

[1] See J. B. Mays, *Education and the Urban Child*, op. cit., especially pp. 133–50, written by Dr Crawford.

[2] David Glass, *et al.*, *Social Mobility in Britain:* Routledge and Kegan Paul, 1954.

do breeding and birth, in the old aristocratic sense, determine future destiny. But this does not mean that a patrician birthright is not still an inestimable advantage. On the contrary, privilege still operates powerfully to maintain the rising generation in the same status and the same income group as its forebears. Professional people, it has been shown, tend to produce children who also follow professional careers.[1] There is an in-breeding, self-selecting process observable in most of the well-paid and highly sought after forms of employment. Medical doctors have sons who become doctors or dentists or lawyers; professors have sons who follow the donnish or similar professional career and bishops reproduce bishops to some extent.

Something like seventy per cent of the nation's children, however, do not receive a grammar or technical school education but proceed to secondary modern schools which the vast majority leave at the statutory age of fifteen without passing an examination or obtaining any paper qualifications whatsoever. As far as future employment prospects go, the children who attend selective schools and have something objective to show prospective employers are the luckier ones. They tend to get the best paid and higher status jobs, while the ex-modern-school boys and girls get what is left to them in the way of skilled work in industry, in manual employment generally, in the retail and distributive trades and in unskilled manual labour.

The educational and economic distinction between the two main groups is largely social in origin. It is society not the schools which dominate the educational system.[2] The grammar schools by and large prepare pupils for middle class ways of living and the modern schools prepare their pupils for traditional working class occupations. It is a distinction between the élite and the crowd, or, sometimes as someone put it much less kindly, between the 'crammed' and the 'damned.' As we have already seen, it is only approximately associated with innate ability and endowment. Who one's parents are, how the home is organised, what sort of family traditions operate, are all very important matters which explain our differential educational and occupational opportunities and achievements.

In recent years some secondary modern schools have been able to encourage a proportion of their keener pupils to stay on after the age of fifteen and some of these boys and girls have been able

---

[1] David Glass, et al., op. cit., p. 441.
[2] See William Taylor, *The Secondary Modern School*, Faber and Faber, 1963.

to take and to pass examinations in subjects at G.C.E. 'O' level. A few of these schools, housed in commodious new premises, complete with uniforms and the other trappings of the grammar schools, are almost indistinguishable from them. The main difference is one of nomenclature. In other words, the grammar school ethos and tradition is almost irrepressible in English secondary education. Because it is so strongly associated with the middle class way of life and its associated occupational aspirations it inevitably appeals to the more ambitious members of society. It meets many of their basic needs and is, as Michael Young has indicated, the royal high road to membership of the meritocracy.[1]

3

During the past hundred years there has been a big increase in the middle classes in this country. This has partly been the cause of, and is also partly the result of, an expansion in secondary education. There is now a large block of middle income people in between the rich and the poor, and there are probably fewer rich people than there used to be and certainly there are far fewer poor than in Victorian times. But it may well be that the period of middle class expansion is coming to an end and that social mobility will tend to be more limited in the future than it has been in the immediate past. What may very well happen—perhaps we can already see it taking place —is that society will be made up of a comparatively small group at the top of the ladder composed of very wealthy and very able people, with the vast majority in the middle ranges, and a small under-privileged, depressed minority at the base. Even in the United States one can see a similar pattern emerging. There, despite the ideological dream of the open society where talent and hard work alone distinguish one citizen from another, sociologists in recent years have convincingly challenged the idea that America is an open and Britain a closed society.[2] It is clear that in both countries class divisions operate, although over here they are more generally accepted and discussed. Hollingshead, for example, showed, on the basis of his study of a Middle Western community of some 10,000 inhabitants in the early 1940's, that there was a close 'functional

[1] Michael Young, *The Rise of the Meritocracy*, Penguin Books, 1961.
[2] C.f. Lipset and Bendix, *Social Mobility in Industrial Society*, Heinemann, 1959, for a stimulating overview of the available data and theories.

relationship between the class position of an adolescent's family and his social behaviour in the community', and that every aspect of the individual's life and his personal aspirations and achievements were closely bound up with his social status.[1] Havighurst and his colleagues, who studied the careers of a generation of boys and girls of a Midwestern River City[2] (population 45,000) also demonstrated that social class differences produced different life chances and histories, although their evidence is certainly not as unequivocal as Hollinghead's. The reason for this may well be that they were dealing with a later decade of children less rigidly tied to family status and more free to do well in school by reason of their basic talents. In other words, the data from the River City research, when compared with the findings at Elmtown, suggests that social changes are at work and that ability is tending to count for more than birth at a time when there is greater equality of opportunity available for all. This means an increased prospect of upward social mobility for some, but it also seems logically to imply a certain amount of downward mobility also.

What appears to be happening as a result of recent social changes in Britain is that there are three, or possibly four, broad groups or types of pupils leaving the schools today. Each group has to be kept in mind in any discussion of young people's behaviour and attitudes. These groups are:

1. Higher class boys and girls, products of public schools and headmasters' conference schools, many of whom pass on to university and especially to Oxbridge colleges.

2. Middle and lower middle class children, educated at grammar and technical schools run by local authorities, some of whom go to Oxbridge while others matriculate to redbrick universities and to other advanced educational institutions.

3. Working class pupils, some from technical and grammar schools but mainly deriving from secondary modern schools, whose only experience of later education is via evening schools, day continuation classes and county colleges, in preparation for skilled and semi-skilled employment, although a proportion go on to teacher training colleges.

---

[1] Hollingshead, op. cit.
[2] Havighurst, *et al.*, *Growing Up in River City*; Wiley, 1962, p. 441.

4. Children from poorer homes and neighbourhoods, ex-pupils of secondary modern and even of unreorganised all-through schools who enter mainly semi-skilled and unskilled employment.

These four categories, of course, overlap (especially one and two) and the pattern is not invariable or immutable. Individuals from any group can turn out to be untypical and rise or fall in the scale. The schema is only useful in a discussion of broad social trends. In particular, any statements about youth need to keep the categories in mind as there is every likelihood that significant differences of outlook will be associated with them. Such an analytical framework, although rough-hewn and open to much qualification, serves to preserve us from the danger of making massive generalisations about contemporary youth which offend against the facts by over-simplification and inclusiveness.

4

The questions of major social interest are how do these three or four groups of school leavers obtain their jobs, what kinds of careers are apparently open to them and what prospects and satisfactions can they be expected to derive from their work in the future. If we understand what actually happens to representatives of the groups we may go a considerable way in the direction of appreciating their problems and sympathising with their difficulties of social adjustment.

We need not say much about group one boys and girls. They are, by and large, well supported by home and well served by their schools. It is possible to criticise these schools on general psychological and philosophical grounds, but of one thing we may be sure; those who have enjoyed a privileged education, however unreal some of its content may be, however outmoded its general ethos and orientation, find their future prospects bright. Many have parents and relatives strategically placed in the political, business, industrial and commercial spheres to effect the necessary introductions and to ease them into substantial posts. The present trend in the recruitment of younger managers seems to be based more on general social and academic qualifications than on the possession of relevant experience in any particular field, least of all, indeed, on having undergone any professional managerial training course. The possessor of an Oxbridge degree, the possessor of any university qualification, indeed, finds himself in a seller's market. He can be comparatively choosy about where he will work and what he will do. He commands a good salary. His position is similar in many ways to the ex-public school boy in the late nineteenth century. The fact that a man had been to Eton or Winchester or Harrow or any of the other big schools was sufficient guarantee of his ability. He automatically belonged to a class of designated leaders who could safely be entrusted by an imperial motherland with the sensible administration of colonial territories and a more or less impartial disciplining of hordes of coloured fags and backward juniors.

Whatever excellent ingredients the older public school system possessed and whatever benefits it bestowed upon nation and empire, it is difficult to believe that such a narrow training is the one most fitted to make good personnel managers, industrial leaders or statesmen, in terms of contemporary realities.[1] The empire has more or less passed away, most of the captains and the kings are long departed. Independent schools often claim to have moved with the times. Their advocates still urge upon us the intrinsic excellence of their methods and blandly point to the fact that their old boys adorn boards of directors, occupy seats in the cabinet, are permanent secretaries in all the most important civil service departments and so on. We are obliged to concede the truth of the facts they point to without necessarily accepting the theory which lies behind these facts. That privilege and power are transmitted down the generations like lands and titles is no new phenomenon. But it does not prove the justice or the efficiency of the arrangement. It may be that the creation of business schools and more vocational training courses for management are called for both by the logic of our changed economic position and by the increasing egalitarianism of our culture. It may be that an Oxbridge or other university degree, the possession of a blue for some juvenile game or another or the fact that a man has been 'capped' for his country does not automatically indicate that he also possesses the skill, imagination and knowledge to be an industrial or political leader or a bureaucratic administrator of the first order. But, however that may be, everyone knows that these are very useful things to have done, very useful qualifications to possess. In England in the mid-nineteen-sixties as in Victorian and Edwardian and Georgian days, if a man wants his son to do well in life he tries to send him to an independent school until he is eighteen

---

[1] Cf. A. D. C. Peterson, *Educating our Rulers*; Duckworth, 1957, for a stimulating essay on this topic.

or more years of age and then on to an Oxbridge college. And this is not only because these schools and colleges offer first rate educational facilities (often indeed the best to be had for the money), but because he 'gets that little something extra' there, the polish, the chance to meet influential people and to acquire the éclat which will stand him in such good stead for the rest of his life.

5

The study of school children's aspirations and expectations is more or less neglected by academic sociologists in this country, although in the U.S.A. some interesting work has been done in this field. Here we have a few limited enquiries mostly into lower class schools and pupils. So far the only attempts that have been made to grapple with children from the top five per cent homes have been carried out by journalists. Our excessive concern with the poor has led us largely to ignore the lives of the rich. Because the latter present few social problems (or cope with them themselves without resource to casework agencies) we tend to ignore them.

In 1959 Godfrey Smith carried out a limited enquiry amongst school leavers in which a proportion of public school pupils were included.[1] Information was obtained from eight boys' public schools, eight boys' grammar schools, eight girls' grammar schools and the same number of technical schools. While they could not be regarded as representative of the country as a whole some interesting and suggestive material was obtained. Mr Smith found a considerable degree of unanimity existing amongst boys at public and grammar schools. In other words the intellectual and social élite of the rising generation had very much the same outlook and shared very similar attitudes and ideas. No less than three-quarters of those who answered the questions wanted to go to a university and in the main their motive was vocational. Public school boys greatly preferred Oxford or Cambridge while grammar school boys, although similarly influenced, were more ready to try other universities.

Girls reacted very similarly to their brothers. More than four in five hoped to enter either university or training college. When they were questioned about their future careers, no less than three-quarters of the boys and four-fifths of the girls knew precisely what they wanted to become. Engineering was the most popular masculine

[1] Godfrey Smith, 'Teenage Aspirations', *The Sunday Times*, 27th Sept., 1959.

career, followed strangely enough by farming. A teaching career
was second in popularity with grammar school pupils but came only
sixth in the public school choices. A career in medicine came third
for both groups and accountancy was a popular choice for both,
although more subscribed to by the independent school pupils
apparently because many had relatives in that profession. Public
school boys favoured a legal career; it came fifth in their order of
preference but was insignificant among the grammar school group.
The latter, however, placed a career in the civil service equal fourth
with accountancy and with science. A naval career was placed seventh
by the independent school scholars but was not mentioned by their
grammar school counterparts.

Technical school boys not surprisingly chose engineering in some
shape or form while a career in one or other of the armed forces
came a very remote second.

Girls from all schools overwhelmingly elected a career in teaching,
with nursing next and medicine third. In the main they tended to
eschew the more glamorised kind of occupation.

Mr Smith summarised the picture of the average boy attending
private or higher selective schools in these terms:

He is, shall we say, sixteen years old. He is conservative, conformist,
very modest, fairly intelligent and rather nice. But he is not by any reach
of the imagination a brilliant talker. He hopes to go to Cambridge and
to be some sort of engineer one day; he hopes to marry and have a comfortable, safe job. No, he certainly does not want to emigrate, he is quite
happy in this country. He loves sport and probably will spend his weekends
playing or watching some game. He would like, within moderation, to
help other people. He is uninterested in politics. On the whole he thinks
religion is a good thing, though he does not want to take an active part
in religion himself. He listens with respect to what his parents and teachers
tell him. He is a little cynical, a shade worldly-wise.

He is not anxious to indulge in any wild adventure himself. He is
depressingly conventional.[1]

As far as getting to the top was concerned, the grammar school
boys (80 per cent) thought hard work the most important factor,
with personality a poor second and influence or luck practically
nowhere.

The public school pupils thought that hard work and personality
were almost equal (48 per cent to 45 per cent) but like their grammar
school coevals placed influence or luck very low in their lists.

[1] Godfrey Smith, 'Teenage Aspirations', *The Sunday Times*, 27th Sept., 1959.

The vast majority agreed that youngsters nowadays had better opportunities than ever before, no doubt echoing their elders' opinion.

The people who carried out the investigation found, though they seriously looked for it, very little indication of bitterness or resentment against adverse influences. The overall picture depressed Mr Smith. An unnamed psychologist who took part in the enquiry put it more objectively but probably meant the same thing when he said:

A drive towards conformity appears more widespread than was supposed amongst the youth of today in this country. Happiness through submerging individuality for the sake of conformity seems to be replacing the protestant ethic of happiness through achievement, involving, in its extreme form, fame or notoriety.[1]

The general portrait presented by the *Sunday Times* enquiry carried out in 1959 agrees in almost every respect with a similar survey carried out in 1956 by Miss Thelma Veness[2] and some of the students of the psychology department at Birkbeck College with a group of 1300 boys and girls who left grammar, technical and secondary modern schools in two English counties.

Miss Veness tried to ascertain what these youngsters wanted to be, to do and to have in the future. The result, while, like that of the *Sunday Times* enquiry, not claiming to be based on a comprehensive investigation of contemporary adolescents, again touched on topics of the widest possible social interest and importance. Several techniques were used varying from written questionnaires to contest analysis of essays, from level of aspiration tests to face to face interviews. The findings were thus as detailed and thorough, reliable and objective as present research methods in such a tricky field permit. But the overall picture of contemporary youth whom Miss Veness leaves us with is far from being exciting or even very attractive. The value of hard work was mentioned by technical pupils in particular but grammar school boys were almost as insistent on the virtuous necessity of training for a job. Boys valued a job chiefly because of its prospects for promotion, high salary or a chance to travel: girls, on the other hand, were less clearly attracted by the same rewards and were as likely to talk about 'being able to keep

[1] Godfrey Smith, 'Teenage Aspirations', *The Sunday Times*, 27th Sept., 1959·
[2] Thelma Veness, *School Leavers, Their Aspirations and Expectations*, Methuen, 1962.

clean and tidy at work' or 'doing good to other people' as to stress
mere financial elements. Marriage and maternity remained for the
girls the central interest and pivot of their lives. Pensions did not
seem to appeal to many of these youngsters in the way that they used
to entice their less secure predecessors in the twenties and thirties.
A safe well-paid job 'somewhere in middle management in industry
or similar status in other occupations or professions' epitomises
the height of their ambitions.

Among the wishes that can be called plans or assumptions, noted in
earlier chapters, are a general state of contentment, or even happiness,
for themselves and for their loved ones; the support, comfort and identity
that is provided by a home and family; money to spend without undue
anxiety; and, especially for boys, the fulfilment of a job that is interesting.[1]

The formula is unexceptionable yet, for all its cosy domesticity,
strikes a little chill to the heart. Somehow it all sounds so humdrum,
so safe and so desperately self-centred. What of the starry-eyed
enthusiasms which we used to associate with youth, the impulsive
espousal of great and often hopeless causes, the soaring idealism?
Money tucked away in the bank, or invested in sound equities, a
snug fireside for a winter's evening, the security of family ties are all
excellent things, but it is a little surprising to find school children
rating them so highly. Whatever value these aspirations possess and
however much they obviously contribute to social stability, they are
certainly not the stuff of which heroic manhood is made. Our
Victorian ancestors would have been appalled by the narrowness of
the horizons thus displayed.

Undoubtedly, however, this widespread desire for security and
tameness is a true reflection of the values held up for emulation by
the parental and adult world.

These are in fact the goals we hold out to young people today and
it is not very surprising to find that most of them accept our evalua-
tions and make them their own.

The picture in America seems to be very similar. Hollingshead, for
example, considered that as far as his Class I and Class II Elmtown
adolescents were concerned in the main they wanted to go into
business at a fairly high level or to become professional people, with
a minority opting for farming.[2] His Class III group were much less

---

[1] Thelma Veness, *School Leavers, Their Aspirations and Expectations*, Methuen,
1962, p. 135.
[2] Hollingshead, op. cit., pp. 282, *et seq.*

inclined towards the higher professional kinds of work (36 per cent as compared with 77 per cent in the two preceding classes), while Class IV showed an even smaller percentage oriented in this direction. His bottom social group, Class V, were almost the reverse of Class II in their outlook, and their socially less established position was further exemplified in the fact that no less than 41 per cent of them had no idea about a vocation at all. Thus we can see how the 'pattern of vocational choices corresponds roughly with the job patterns associated with each class in the adult work world.'[1] A certain realism, then, may be said to underlie the judgement of young Elmtowners in their assessments of their own future prospects, a realism perhaps tainted with a certain amount of inertia and cynicism.

This realistic appraisal of one's own life chances has been well illustrated more recently in the results of a study by F. M. Katz in which the aspirations and eventual jobs obtained by a group of four hundred or so English boys were compared.[2] It was found that 78 per cent actually obtained the precise jobs that they had expected, which either means that their self-assessments were remarkably sound or, more likely, that their ambitions were rather too modest.

There are, of course, the nonconformists who still look for more hazardous and venturesome ways of spending their days, but the fact has to be admitted that nowadays, in spite of all that so-called adventure courses, Outward Bound Schools and Duke of Edinburgh Awards can do to the contrary, such youngsters are the exceptions. The days of our pioneering are over and it is no good trying to behave as though they were not. Another depressing feature which seemed to characterise the conforming majority that Miss Veness studied is the more or less passive manner in which the majority of these boys and girls seemed to accept other people's judgements on them as final. Examination results tended to be taken on their face value as true measures of ability and indices of future success. Too many of these youngsters were prepared to write themselves off as being merely ordinary or below average folk, or, to use their own language as 'not having many brains.'

Judged on the scale of ambitiousness the products of grammar and technical schools scored more highly than those at secondary modern schools.

---

[1] Hollingshead, op cit., p. 285.
[2] F. M. Katz, *Journal of Social Psychology*, vol. 57.

Thus children who are categorised at an early age as being o
lesser academic ability henceforth see themselves in this light an
tailor their personal aspirations thereafter with becoming modesty
Such attitudes, as I have already suggested, may make for socia
stability but is hardly likely to contribute to national greatness i
the old sense.

Professor Mace, in an admirable preface to Miss Veness' book
summed up the significance of the principal findings by suggestin
that 'Some new thinking is clearly needed about the ways and mean
of encouraging reasonable ambitions.'[1] An ideology of limite
success is not good enough for a nation which wishes to contribut
to the future development of civilisation. Conformity with the officia
values of our society will not inject sufficient dynamism and idealisn
to promote the kind of changes and reconstruction discussed in th
final section of this book. The quality of education is crucial for th
future. A nation of pedestrians is hardly likely to find itself at th
van of progress in the twenty-first century.

In a more recent and smaller study of two hundred secondary
modern boys and girls in Sheffield, Mr M. P. Carter has underline
the importance of the local culture and the influence of the family
in forming youngster ideas about what work to choose.[2]

The work of the schools is seen by comparison to be secondary t
these wider and deeper local influences in shaping children's futur
destinies.[3] Nevertheless, 'the largest group of parents consisted o
those who allowed their children free-will in choice of work.'[4] Thi
seemed to be particularly true of the less ambitious lower workin
class families where the parents often 'abrogated responsibility fo
helping the child to come to a decision, and accepted whateve
choice was made,'[5] on the basis, more often than not, of nothing
more substantial than the children's own ignorance.

These Sheffield school children were influenced in their jot
choices more by the idea of 'the joys to be derived from new clothes,
travel and entertainments' than by sheer interest in the work involved
'To keep up with one's friends, and to entertain the girl friend in the
way to which she has become accustomed'[6] demanded ready cash

[1] Veness, op. cit., p. xxiii. [2] Carter, op. cit.
[3] Cf. James S. Coleman, *The Adolescent Society*; Free Press, 1961, p. 140 *et.
seq.*, 'When forced to a choice between best friend, favourite teacher, and
parents, almost no one chose teacher, while the choices were about equally split
between friend and parents.'
[4] Ibid., p. 92. [5] Ibid., p. 93. [6] Ibid., p. 112.

which in turn meant work. Work for them was hence in the main a source of money—both parents and children assumed this—and all ideas of vocationalism and satisfaction to be derived from work seemed to be unrealistic and remote. Yet the large majority did not seem to be motivated by any desire to get higher wages or much more remunerative jobs: 'they would be satisfied with "reasonable" pay—about the same as other people get,'[1] but they would, however, try to avoid jobs for which wages were unusually low. For this reason apprenticeships were not highly sought after. Carter's findings for these lower class school leavers is in sharp contrast with Godfrey Smith's results from his enquiry amongst children coming from a greater variety of social backgrounds. Only one-fifth of Carter's secondary modern boys thought in terms of future prospects and wanted to be more than 'ordinary workers,' whereas future prospects of obtaining well paid and secure high status employment was a major motivating force with Smith's sample of boys. Carter's girls were interested in 'having nice people to work with' and 'having the opportunity to meet people' but were not much concerned about security. Work for the girls was obviously not thought of in terms of being a life's career at all, but rather as a prelude to marriage and a means of supplementing the family income whenever convenient.

Professor Ferguson followed the careers of a generation of Glasgow school-boys over a three year period, from January 1947 to January 1950, in an endeavour to ascertain how a representative sample of 'normal' youngsters fared so that valid comparisons could be made with those suffering from physical or social handi-caps.[2] All left school at the age of fourteen and there were no grammar or high school pupils in the sample. Ferguson found that 'Four-fifths of the boys knew on leaving school what they wanted to do. Two-thirds desired manual work, usually skilled; $11 \cdot 3$ per cent wished to take up non-manual work, mostly in the distributive trades or in offices.'[3]

He noted that 'The higher the level of scholastic performance and of home assessment, the greater the proportion of boys who desired skilled manual work.'[4] He also discovered that 'the reason most frequently given for job-preference on leaving school was "the inter-

---

[1] James S. Coleman, *The Adolescent Society*; Free Press, 1961, p. 113.
[2] Thomas Ferguson and James Cunnison, *The Young Wage-Earner*, published for The Nuffield Foundation by the Oxford University Press, 1951.
[3] Ibid., p. 9.   [4] Ibid., pp. 9–10.

est of the work", which accounted for half of the expressed prefer-
ences,' and that second, 'a long way behind came parents' wish,
with still farther behind, the boy's desire for ultimate position and
good wages in that order.'[1]

In so far as he found that 'interest of the work was the chief
motivating agent among boys of all levels of scholastic ability' his
results are at variance with Carter's. The Glaswegian school leavers,
despite their working class background, did not look upon work
merely as a means to an end but were prepared to find some intrinsic
personal satisfaction in its performance. The differential findings of
these two very interesting enquiries may, of course, merely be a
result of different culture patterns. It may well be that there is, or,
at least, was in the not far distant past, a tradition for enjoyment in
work which is part and parcel of the Scottish way of life. Another
possible explanation for the difference could be found in a changed
attitude to work and to life in a comparatively more affluent period.
Carter's boys are a decade younger than Ferguson and Cunnison's
and they may well have been subject to a number of significantly
changed social influences. The newer attitude of the Sheffield boys
which regards work as little more than a necessary means to acquire
money for enjoyment and good living may signify an important
social change which in the years following the cessation of the Second
World War seems to have become endemic in several European
countries.

In his penetrating essay in which he analyses the new type of
young worker today, who passes his life in a more or less atomised
and empty world in spite of high living standards, Karl Bednarik
has drawn attention to a similar trend.[2] The *Schlurf*, as Bednarik
calls him, a type in the Weberian sense, is found in all social strata
in post-war Austria and is by no means exclusive to the working
class. The young worker today springs from and represents a state
of mind rather than a class; he is an atmospheric rather than ideological phenomenon. The new affluence and its associated cultural
banality has eliminated the concept of worker in the traditional
Marxist sense. He is an anti-type rather than a simple type, an
ersatz personality enjoying what Bednarik calls 'freedom at zero', i.e.
the mainly empty freedom of the 'purely formal ego'. Nurtured in

---

[1] Thomas Ferguson and James Cunnison, *The Young Wage-Earner*, p. 10.
[2] Karl Bednarik, *The Young Worker Today: A New Type*, ed. J. P. Mayer,
translated by R. Tupholme; Faber & Faber, 1953.

the welfare state and being a member of what Bednarik graphically calls 'the Town-Hall Young', he nevertheless exists in a world of 'perpetual fictitious want'. He pursues pleasure as in a dream and seeks to humanise the functionalisation of every aspect of life resulting from the development of modern techniques by addiction to dancing and the illusionism of the cinema. Had he been writing today no doubt Bednarik would have included television in his list of illusionist pastimes.

The *Schlurf* exists in a spiritual vacuum. In the spiritual sense he is a dead-end kid, a left over from a culture which has moved a long, long way from its origin and roots,

> Wandering between two worlds, one dead
> The other powerless to be born.

6

While we may not wish to follow Bednarik too far into his intuitively based and often tendentious analysis of the contemporary young worker, we would do well to consider the possibility that a basic change has come over modern society's attitude towards work which may no longer involve either the craftsman's pride in personal achievement nor spring from the Protestant ethical viewpoint of labour as an inevitable means of religious salvation. Carter's youngsters may well evidence a change in the direction of a new attitude towards work as being little more than a necessary evil or interruption of pleasurable experiences. Kirk Dansereau, commenting on the fact that in American society young people are more and more tending to be cut off from the real business of the adult world, has suggested that 'the teenager's design for living, organised as it is around leisure-time pursuits and fun, rather than around work, may be a prototype of the adult world of the future when automation has deprived many people of work—as adult patterns have for so long deprived teenagers—as a source of life satisfaction.'[1]

Coleman argues in his important book, *The Adolescent Society*, that teenagers in the U.S.A. are now so committed to a different and distinct way of life that, as far as youth is concerned, '. . . society is confronted no longer with a set of individuals to be trained towards adulthood, but with distinct *social systems*, which offer a united

[1] H. Kirk Dansereau, 'Work and the Teen-Ager'; *Annals* of the American Academy of Political and Social Science, Nov. 1961.

front to the overtures made by adult society.'[1] This teen-age culture is not merely inward-looking and characteristically focused upon itself, it is also extremely sport-oriented and pleasure seeking. Groups of young people hence tend to form their own sets of teen-age sub-societies 'which focus teen-age interests and attitudes on things far removed from adult responsibilities, and which may develop standards that lead away from those goals established by the larger society.'[2] Adolescents, hence, are not only largely cut off from the main branch of social life, they are also following different goals of a more nakedly hedonistic nature.

If this is the prototype of the adult world of the future it is certainly not likely to be outstandingly the arena of responsible social action and of thoughtful individual choice. Nothing, in fact, could ultimately be more demoralising than an effective divorce between work and recreation, and it may well be that one of the deep causes of adolescent unrest and frustration in the U.S.A. stems from their being obliged to live a life almost wholly dedicated to play and to similar unrealities.

If the pressures of social changes, which invariably manifest themselves at an early stage in the behaviour of the more youthful and impressionable members of the community, are minimising the idea of work as something of an end in itself or as a spiritual value reinforced by strong religious sanctions, it will no longer do to criticise the young if their attitudes are more in harmony with a contemporary rather than a traditional outlook. Work and play, fun and money-making, are therefore seen to be functionally associated. The sense of vocation is fading just as the notion of craftsmanship has most obviously passed away. We begin to see more clearly what Hoggart meant when he described youngsters today as 'ground between the millstones of technocracy and democracy' as members of a society which 'gives them almost limitless freedom of the sensations, but makes few demands on them—the use of their hands and of a fraction of their brains for forty hours a week.'[3] A reduction in working hours, an increase in leisure time exposes them to an ever increasing degree to the lures of 'the entertainers and their efficient mass-equipment.'

We are, hence, led to the conclusion that school is duo-functional. It is basically appreciated as a preparation for work, to enable the

[1] Coleman, op. cit., p. 4. Author's italics.   [2] Ibid., p. 9.
[3] Hoggart, op. cit., p. 204.

individual to compete for a job and to earn his own living. It is also a preparation for non-working hours, for training in the utilisation of leisure. It is concerned therefore to be both vocational and recreational or therapeutic; it must fit children for the most suitable jobs, and it must try also to help them to use their leisure time, both now and in the years ahead, wisely and creatively.

The school, like the youth organisation, is to be thought of, then, as a fundamental part of what Leonard Barnes once, speaking more specifically of the youth organisations, called a 'cultural health service.'[1]

These two objectives, while not inevitably dichotomous, are nevertheless, difficult to achieve simultaneously. Concentration on the bread and butter end of the curriculum and on good examination performance gives the more utilitarian school an advantage over the one which aims to present a broadly based syllabus incorporating non-vocational subjects. Boys from the former type of school may do better or rather obtain more marks than their counterparts from the more liberal and 'progressive' schools and so in a highly competitive age do better in the worldly sense, although as people their lives may be the narrower and their personalities less adequately developed. In older days, when privilege and money bought secondary education more or less as a matter of course, more time and attention could be given to aspects of the curriculum of a purely aesthetic or generally cultural kind, without, in the main, running much risk of seriously handicapping pupils chances of getting 'good' jobs later. Nowadays the competition is much more fierce at every educational level. Artistic, aesthetic and personality-enriching subjects are steadily being shouldered aside by a rising generation who are much more concerned with science and engineering and much less interested in poetry and the political principles of the Greek city state. Without entering into the two cultures controversy, associated with Sir Charles Snow's well-known criticisms, it is well to point out that at grammar school and again at university level there is a real danger of education becoming over-vocationalised and specific to the detriment of all round personality development, while, at the other end of the scale, the secondary modern school (so soundly based on sane educational theory) is tending to exaggerate the general at the expense of the vocational elements, eager to

---

[1] Leonard Barnes, *The Outlook for Youth Work*, King George's Jubilee Trust, 1948.

give a thorough training in 'social competence' which unfortunately carries little weight in the job market.

Schools are not really free institutions at all. They cannot follow the broad highway of general educational development without, at the same time, exposing their pupils to various future disadvantages. Paper qualifications become more important each decade, not only for admission to the seats of higher learning and for all kinds of clerical employment but also for apprenticeships to most skilled and even to some semi-skilled jobs. Growing lack of esteem for some white collar posts of the merely clerical, pen-pushing kind coupled with higher rewards for manual workers have transformed our attitude to the social status of certain occupations and dispelled many former prejudices about the inferiority of vocationalism. Universities, grammar and technical schools, in fact any teaching institutions which provide successful candidates with formal quali- fications at the end of the course, are truly vocational in nature. The bachelor of arts degree has a long history as indicating a man's fitness to teach. Snobberies and all, the public schools always were royal roads to the higher status occupations. The grammar schools, too, have always fitted scholars for the more rewarding kinds of employment. The secondary modern school which, by and large, sends its *alumni* forth without any formal qualifications or certificates must expect that its boys and girls will, in bulk, have to be content with whatever is left for them in the job market.

While they have been busily and conscientiously pursuing lofty educational principles they have, at the same time, been fitting their products for the lower paid and less highly esteemed occupations. What constitutes a 'good' school is in fact determined by society not by educationists. This is the bitter lesson that school teachers and parents and eventually the pupils themselves have to learn. To do well in a competitive society means having the edge on the other candidate, having something tangible to waft in the face of a pros- pective employer or appointing committee. It is a great pity that this is so, but little good will come of refusing to face facts merely because they are unpleasant and an affront to pure pedagogic theory.

7

It is in the light of such general social facts that we have to consider the whole field of what has rather misleadingly come to be known professionally as vocational guidance. As far as the run of the mill school leavers go, the task of imparting this vocational guidance is entrusted to the Youth Employment Officers who are usually but not always attached to the local educational authority. Before the second world war, only some 30 per cent of the job placings were handled by the juvenile employment officers of the Ministry of Labour. Today the majority of school leavers come into touch with the local Youth Employment Officers. The common practice appears to be for the officers to visit the schools before the final year pupils are due to leave. They have a talk with pupils and, in schools which invite them, with their parents, with a view to finding out what kind of job would be most suitable, bearing in mind such factors as school records of conduct and attainment. Presumably the Y.E.O.'s take the state of the local market into consideration and the types of vacancies that have been notified to the bureau. It is important to realise that by no means all employers wish to make use of the service and that there are many firms offering good career prospects which prefer to recruit by personal recommendation and application. One result of this is that the Y.E.O. often receives a disproportionate number of less attractive jobs which the employers know they will have some difficulty in filling. But this is by no means always the case. Practice varies from place to place, and depends to a considerable extent on the vitality of the links forged between the officers administering the service and the local employers of labour.

The task of vocational guidance has been well epitomised by Dr Fleming as the problem of how 'to match job analysis with personal analysis in such a way that, through the fullest possible functioning, each individual may contribute most fully to the welfare of the group and secure most readily the personal satisfactions consequent upon such contribution.'[1] To which, I imagine, the veteran of the youth employment service would wryly retort, 'Precisely, but how is it to be done?'

There is indeed no welfare department quite so impotent as Youth Employment, for it cannot create the jobs which its clients are most capable of filling and, unlike the Ministry of Labour, it cannot train its clients to fill such vacancies as exist. As a result of the fact that it seeks to administer a service in a field in which it has no control, it can degenerate into nothing more than a rather soulless

[1] C. M. Fleming, *Adolescence, Its Social Psychology*, 2nd edn. (revised), Routledge and Kegan Paul, 1963, p. 188.

juvenile job-filling agency, sending bevies of boys and girls clutching
cards in their hands to present themselves before potential employers,
and hoping that at least one of their number will prove acceptable.[1]
In times of rising juvenile unemployment too, its position becomes
fairly desperate. More and more it takes on the task of job filling
and less and less can afford to offer a professional vocational
guidance service. At the present time, as is well known, there are
indications in certain parts of the country, especially in the North
East, on Clydeside and in the North West, of increasing unemployment both amongst adults and juveniles. In such areas the work
of the Y.E.O.s must be extremely depressing.

Vocational guidance remains more or less an unfulfilled ideal in
many if not in all areas. In his Sheffield study, for instance, Carter
concluded that the Service did not 'loom large in children's minds
immediately prior to leaving school not even as a job-finding agency,'
and further he discovered that 'after their School-leaving Interviews,
most children soon forgot about the Service.'[2] At that time more
personal and informal methods of finding employment were in the
ascendency. He found that not only did few of the large firms
notify the bureau of engineering apprenticeships but that a great
many parents had the mistaken idea that only second rate jobs
were ever notified to the agency—a criticism which his evidence
refuted. Only 27 per cent of the Sheffield school leavers who were
studied obtained their first jobs via the Y.E.S. as compared with about
35 per cent who got their jobs by friends' or relatives' assistance.[3]
Moreover, chance calls at firms were successful in no less than 17
per cent of the cases. Of the thirty-one boys and twenty-three girls
who were placed initially by the Y.E.S., half of the boys and almost
as many of the girls left during the first twelve months. Comparing
this outcome with those who obtained their work privately, Carter
comments: 'Measured by the number of subsequent changes, then,
help from the Y.E.O. proved to be no better a method of finding
employment than any other method, and a much worse method than
most: most of the jobs notified to the Y.E.O. have a high rate of
turnover—the work is not attractive.'[4]

Miss Veness's enquiry is disappointingly thin on the topic of the
Youth Employment Service but she does indicate that, in their last
year at school, children seemed to become more aware of the

[1] Cf. Carter, op. cit., p. 167.   [2] Ibid., p. 161.   [3] Ibid., p. 164.
[4] Ibid., p. 169.

officers' presence, although only 'between a quarter and a half underlined this source of information' concerning likely future employment.[1] Leslie Wilkins' investigation carried out in 1950 with 1,400 boys and 450 girls between the ages of fifteen and nineteen years for the Central Office of Information revealed, in answer to the question 'How did you hear that your first job was vacant?', that 25 per cent of the boys first heard through the Ministry of Labour or the Youth Employment Service as compared with 26 per cent as a result of personal enquiry, 26 per cent from relatives and friends, 7 per cent in answer to advertisements and 8 per cent via their schools.[2] The picture for the girls was very similar, the only difference being that they more often heard about the vacancies through schools and advertisements, a finding which was partly accounted for by the tradition in the trades concerned.[3]

There is a general agreement amongst those who have studied the Y.E.S. that much remains to be done before it constitutes the kind of service that was envisaged by its initiators. A working party convened by The King George Jubilee Trust recommended *inter alia* that an extension of the employer's responsibilities should 'include reporting to the Youth Employment Service the entry and discharge of all young people under 18,' but was definitely opposed to the idea of obliging all young people to seek employment solely through the service.[4] It recommended better training qualifications for the officers but did not make it clear exactly how further professional training would be likely to make their work very much more effective in a purely voluntary system. Miss Veness suggested that the Y.E.O.'s might be given 'greater scope' by being permitted to 'enter the schools earlier, to extend their acquaintance with each boy and girl over a longer period and to allot more than the ten or twenty minutes now available for giving advice and help in most important decisions.'[5] To do this, she thought, the service would need further resources and manpower.

[1] Veness, op. cit., pp. 74–75.

[2] Ferguson and Cunnison, op. cit., found in their study of Glasgow school leavers in the nineteen-forties that 12 per cent of the boys found their first job with the help of the Employment Exchange.

[3] L. T. Wilkins, *The Adolescent in Britain*; The Social Survey, Central Office of Information, 1955, pp. 31–32.

[4] *Citizens of Tomorrow*, King George's Jubilee Trust, 1955.

[5] Veness, op. cit., pp. 170–71.

Carter pointed out, as a result of his researches, that 'Vocational guidance is, properly, a continuous process: it is as important for a child to receive guidance when seeking subsequent jobs as when he is first starting work.'[1] Contact with youngsters after they have left school and wish to change their jobs is inevitably a chancy affair. The bureau can do little more than invite young people to return for further consultations. Whether or not this difficulty could be overcome is doubtful in the present circumstances but until it is we would do well to remember Carter's judgment that 'the Y.E. Service is at present not fulfilling this role any more adequately than its task of counselling school leavers.'[2] At times of full employment, when there are more vacancies than applicants, the task of vocational guidance may prove to be more viable, but, generally speaking, at the moment it remains more of an ideal than a reality.

8

A topic closely related to that of vocational guidance and one which constantly crops up in the day to day work of the advisor on employment is that of entering a so-called skilled job via a recognised apprenticeship. Many youngsters are misled into thinking they are serving an apprenticeship when in fact they are doing nothing of the sort. They are merely doing some of the simple tasks and chores for skilled or semi-skilled adult workers and there is no question of them serving their time and becoming journeymen after an agreed number of years. One thing is very obvious and that is that there are far more school leavers who wish to enter a skilled occupation than openings can be found for them. The pressure to get into an apprenticeship of some sort is very strong, and this, be it marked, in spite of the generally recognised fact that the boys will get much smaller pay packets than those who initially opt for unskilled manual work with its earlier and more immediate financial rewards. There is no dearth of demand for apprenticeships. But there sometimes is a shortage of suitably qualified candidates on the one hand and a lack of openings in local firms on the other. The rapidly increasing birth rate since the end of the last war which first produced the bulge and still produces annually a bumper crop of babies, together with the swing towards staying longer at school has produced in recent years what we can only call 'the apprenticeship crisis.' Several

[1] Carter, op. cit. p. 170. [2] Ibid.

reports have studied this problem; government committees representing various interests have been set up to study the facts and make recommendations for future policy.

The Carr Committee reported in 1958 that existing facilities for apprenticeship training were inadequate in quantity and in some cases in quality.[1] They tended to regard Industry as being responsible for making the necessary facilities available but said little about the task of the schools, apart from a pious wish for closer collaboration between industrialists and those in charge of further education which went no further than sitting on one another's committees. The alleged shortage of skill, or, rather, of openings in skilled employment, is seen nowadays, not merely as a personal problem but also, as something of a potential threat to the future national economy. In order to maintain our expanding internal economy and preserve our current standard of living, so the argument runs, we must export more and more manufactured goods. This, in turn, depends on a number of factors, one of which is the availability of a comparatively mobile, technically flexible and skilled labour force. There is likely to be a smaller and smaller demand for sheer muscle and brawn in the years ahead. Prospects for manual labourers who have no technical competence, therefore, grow less and less each generation. It is in everybody's interest hence that we should turn ourselves as quickly as possible into a highly trained, well-educated democracy. The problem is how to get more skill and what factors present obstacles to this desired development.

Ferguson and Cunnison showed in their follow up study of the generation of Glaswegian school leavers that there was, in the late nineteen-forties at any rate, a marked falling away in skill as time went on.[2] This was particularly marked amongst those boys whose careers had been disturbed by the compulsory period of two years' national service which was then in force. 346 of the survey group went into the Services, while 222 were rejected on various grounds and remained at home. The group who were called up were on the whole physically and in other ways superior to those who were rejected, yet by the time they were twenty-two it was found that

[1] *Training For Skill*, Report by a Subcommittee of the National Joint Advisory Council on the Recruitment and Training of Young Workers in Industry, H.M.S.O., 1958.
[2] T. Ferguson and J. Cunnison, *In Their Early Twenties*, published for the Nuffield Foundation by the Oxford University Press, 1956.

more of them had drifted away from skilled work than was the case with their less able contemporaries who had not experienced the upheaval of call up. Only 59 per cent of those who had been in skilled employment at the age of seventeen were still in skilled work five years later, and the investigators put this retreat from skill down to the interruption and unsettlement consequent upon having to spend two years in the armed forces. Now that conscription has ended, we may assume that this particular problem will be reduced. Nevertheless, their study illustrates how easily even the better type of boys can be deflected from following a tradesman's career and how important it is to maintain young people's contact with skilled employment uninterruptedly during the decade subsequent to leaving school.

Generally speaking, two stock answers have been given to the question 'Why are we so short of skilled people?' One stresses the restrictions on recruitment imposed by the unions in self-defence against possible depression of status and lower financial rewards resulting from a surplus of men for available jobs. The other attributes the shortage to a lack of desire on the part of youngsters themselves to undergo the necessary period of training. Lady Williams has effectively demolished both these explanations.[1] Although there are some trades which too drastically limit the intake of apprentices (e.g. printing), the majority of unions during the post-war boom period have not enforced stringent conditions for admission. Moreover the idea that insufficient youngsters want to enter skilled employment will not hold water. Every Youth Employment Officer knows that the demand far outruns the supply of available apprenticeships.

The chief reason for the shortage of skill, as Lady Williams has demonstrated, is to be found in the enormous change which has taken place in industry and employment in recent years. The lower birthrates of the depressed thirties has resulted in shortage of young workers. Unskilled work has temporarily offered enticingly high wages and, in order to compete effectively, employers of apprentices have been obliged to offer a much higher remuneration compared with what they used to offer pre-war. Not only are they obliged to pay their apprentices more but they are also required to give them

[1] Gertrude Williams, *Recruitment to Skilled Trades*; Routledge and Kegan Paul, 1957: and *Training for Skill*; Fabian Research Pamphlet, No. 205, 1959.

day release to attend continuation classes at the local technical college. Small and medium sized firms find this an almost intolerable imposition. Far from being the source of cheap labour that they used to be, apprentices nowadays have become an additional burden which only the more affluent and larger and far-sighted firms have, on the whole, been willing to accept.

The crux of the apprenticeship problem is seen then to be one of agreeing who pays for the training; the employer or the community? Firms who train apprentices complain that non-training firms poach them just as soon as they qualify. Furthermore, there is a growing consensus within industry which argues that training for skilled work is an educational matter and should fall within the province of the schools. On the other hand, many educators put forward the converse argument to the effect that schools cannot be narrowly vocational and that industry should be willing to take responsibility for equipping its own recruits at its own expense. Radical rethinking is obviously called for and considerations of tradition and sectional interests will not solve the problem for us. Among recent experiments which perhaps foreshadow the future are certain American schemes involving apprenticeship, not to a particular firm, but to the industry as a whole—an attractive idea which overcomes the disadvantages of the smaller and poorer firms, on the one hand, and, on the other, is calculated to ensure an adequate supply of trained personnel for the entire industry concerned. An increased use of 'sandwich' courses is perhaps a more likely solution in Britain. This would involve releasing more and more youngsters for longer periods of formal instruction at local colleges with the result, one should hope, that they would receive an altogether more efficient level of teaching. This would not only bring the educational authorities into closer and closer contact with industry, but would also go a long way towards ensuring that skill has a more or less uniform meaning so that the status of being a skilled craftsman could depend more upon actual proficiency than upon merely 'serving your time' by doing odd jobs about the shop as so often it did in the past and still does today in some employment.

Whatever remedies and policies finally emerge, there can be no doubt whatsoever that the problem of increasing the pool of skilled workers is one of the most urgent tasks facing us as a nation today. Upon its successful solution depends not only the maintenance of a reasonable standard of living for the vast majority of citizens, but also the psychological adjustment of the rising generation for whom work, to be dignified and personally rewarding, must have a meaning other than money-making.

9

Before leaving the topic it is perhaps desirable to say something about what is currently called adjustment to work or initiation into industry. It is something of a fetish to stress the difficulties of passing from what is often thought of as the sheltered world of school to the rough and tumble existence of workshop and factory. What is altogether too often forgotten is that, as far as many of these youngsters are concerned, the last day at school is heralded with a sigh of relief and the first day at work welcomed with gusto. M. P. Carter in his study of a selection of Sheffield school leavers is especially interesting in his discussion of this whole business of the young person's adjustment to the ethos of working life.[1] Some youngsters, he admits, are apprehensive about giving up the status of pupil and assuming that of worker. One suspects, moreover, that some teachers unconsciously encourage this reaction, for many of them may actually be very ignorant of what working in a shop, office, or factory really entails. But whatever inward misgivings the youngsters may experience, it is abundantly clear from Mr Carter's enquiry that most of them look forward to work, however dull it may seem to be, as something likely to be much more rewarding than school life. 'You haven't always got someone hanging round your neck, telling you what to do, and bickering at you,' declared one of the Sheffield group.

'And you don't have to ask anyone if you want to go to the toilet,' he added.[2] Furthermore, although at work they expected to be kept much harder at it than they had ever been in school, there was at least the compensation of the pay packet to look forward to at the end of the week. The constant indignity of being personally assessed and tested is also a thing of the past once the school gates are left behind. 'At work,' said a Sheffield respondent, 'you may be good, bad, average, or mediocre—but people do not keep telling you so.'[3]

Teachers, of course, tend to grow uneasy when they hear such comments and the implied criticisms. They are apt to retort defen-

[1] Carter, op. cit., pp. 68–87.   [2] Ibid., p. 73.
[3] Ibid., p. 74.

sively by saying that the same boys who complain about being bossed around at school and claim to enjoy being treated more as an adult at work are often the very ones who are most resistant to learning, the ones who idle in class and generally in their own language 'play around a lot.' This is, indeed, true enough and one has no desire to use the off-the-cuff comments of youngsters as anything more than indices of potential disharmony. But there is a fair amount of evidence to suggest that the last year or years of school life are not being handled as wisely as they might be. The increased incidence of juvenile delinquency in the final year of formal education is a phenomenon which the authors of the Crowther Report drew our attention to, suggesting that this in-between-times produces stresses and strains for children which are not being adequately met by either pedagogic or parental assistance.[1]

Perhaps the concern which has been expressed about the first few weeks at work and the dangers of contamination from older workmates, however real these perils may be, have served to obscure the wider issue of how and when and over what period of time the whole social transitional process from juvenile to near adult status ought to take place. We have already quoted Carter's comment that 'vocational guidance is, properly, a continuous process.'[2] In making that remark, however, he was thinking more in terms of continuing contact between social welfare officers and young workers throughout the job-getting and job-changing cycle than of Dr Wall's much more thoroughgoing idea of a much earlier contact between the Youth Employment Service and the schools. Dr Wall expressed concern about the lateness of the hour at which the child and his parents often begin to consider the sort of job he will try for, and, as a possible remedy to this, has suggested that a proportion of the time 'might well be devoted, throughout the secondary stage of education, to helping children progressively to gain an insight into the way men earn their living and that this insight should be based upon some actual experience of different kind of jobs and the demands they make.'[3]

What Dr Wall is suggesting might, if carefully carried out, bring that touch of reality, to the secondary modern school at least, which seems to be so necessary for youngsters' social adjustment. 'Rarely or never,' he points out, 'is the whole process of vocational

[1] *15 to 18*, op. cit.   [2] Carter, op. cit., p. 170.
[3] W. D. Wall, *Child of our Times*, op. cit., p. 99.

guidance, induction to work and training considered to be a logical, integral part of education, at least from the beginning of the secondary stage; still less do we see guidance and curriculum as reciprocal functions with an aim set well beyond the confines of full-time education.'[1]

The point is well made and well worth making. Since work occupies one of the major portions of a man's entire lifetime, surely preparation for it and introduction to it ought to figure prominently in any school syllabus? In any case it is obviously wrong to leave it until only two or three terms of school life remain before taking any action.

10

One further aspect of the business of coming to terms with society may briefly be touched upon here; that is a young person's attitude towards politics and his gradual realisation of himself as a responsible citizen called on to take an active or, at least, a not merely passive part in the administration of local and national affairs. It is a topic which is often ignored and overlooked in most books about young people with the result that we are apt to think of training for future citizenship solely in terms of being law-abiding and conscientious at work. But clearly a parliamentary democracy needs to go much further than that in educating its future citizens.

Neither Miss Veness nor Mr Carter deals specifically with young people's political concepts and attitudes. We are to presume from this that either young people have none worth considering or these particular authors felt obliged to ignore this aspect of their lives. Few American researchers have been more concerned about teenagers' notions of how society is and ought to be governed. For example Robert Havighurst and his colleagues in their most enthralling River City enquiry nevertheless define 'adult competence' as involving no more than youngsters becoming in the fullness of time 'successful workers, parents, husbands, wives and homemakers.'[2] This is the way they find young people defining their own ideas of adult competence and the authors appear to be content with this rather restricted interpretation of the concept.

1 W. D. Wall, *Child of our Times*, op. cit., p. 99.
2 R. Havighurst *et. al.*, *Growing Up in River City*, op. cit.; especially pp. 154–61.

There is a curious difference in the democracies about discussing politics. Above all it should never get tangled up with education. Both politics and religion are educationally more or less taboo. They can be taken for granted but not discussed. Schools have Religious Education periods and corporate worship but seldom get down to the fundamentals of belief and disbelief. So, too, with regard to politics, it is taken for granted that one is a patriot in the primitive sense, that one's country is usually in the right, that 'democracy' is the highest form of government known to mankind and the United Nations should be supported within reason, and there it ends.

Except, of course, in sixth forms in grammar schools where debates and free-ranging speculations are often encouraged for the more intellectual and older pupils. But, for the bulk of the nation's school children, in Britain at any rate, we take politics and religion as gently and obliquely as possible. There is, of course, a danger of indoctrination in the tenets of one particular party or sectarian group taking place, and this we would all be against in state run schools. At the same time it is possible to overdo this *noli tangere* notion. And this may be one of the root causes for the political apathy which is so frequently said to characterise modern youth. Godfrey Smith's sample of school leavers did not appear to have any particular interest in politics, let alone ever think of it as a possible future career. Even when they were asked to choose a career to correspond with 'their wildest dreams,' only a handful mentioned being a politician.

I have found myself, in tutoring university social science students, many of whom are destined for careers in social work and industry, that very few of them ever take political principles or practical political realities into consideration when discussing any kind of social or communal problem. For a nation as politically experienced and competent as ours, there is baffling degree of avoidance of controversial matters at school and academic level. Furthermore, in debates on the iniquities of the 11 plus examination or the wastage of talent arising from an unequal educational system, critics usually stress the lack of individual opportunity, the obstacles in the way of private advancement as the most deplorable aspect of the matter and seldom discuss the political principles involved. They seem to be more concerned with equality of opportunity than with the creation of a truly free and equal society as such.

Little wonder, then, if sometimes young people who, in any case, are deemed unworthy of voting until they reach the age of twenty-one plus, are either cynical about or merely uninterested in political issues. Bednarik in a text from which I have already quoted is deeply concerned about the way in which the young workers of post-war Austria avoid political commitment. In the past, he points out, 'In socialism man "found" himself to a certain extent: he found his status as a social being completely dependent on society.'[1] Not so today. Socialism has lost its power and virtue. It has 'ceased to be the "church" of modern man, it no longer wields any spiritual power over men's souls, but only power over their physical needs; it has become a sort of insurance company for the standard of living.' The young workmen of today, Bednarik found, 'seem to congregate in places which are removed from political control and influence,'[2] preferring the pursuit of sensations of pleasure to devotion to the cause which moved their fathers' and forefathers' hearts.

This is not because they underestimate the powers and importance of the state. Rather it is because they think of it as so 'unshakable' and 'unassailable' that 'few attempts are made to resist it.' The state is felt to be outside their power to influence or reshape.

Its emotional impact on their minds is hence totalitarian and depersonalising. So working life tends to lack an ethos, and the pursuit of the moment of pleasure or the purely personal good life takes on prime importance. The affluent generation, which has probably more autonomy than its forerunners ever dreamed of, dissipates its dreams and aspirations in creating not a better society but a happier home for its children. The younger ones are entirely immersed in the world of personal relationships while their parents are bemused by the notion of 'the make-believe paradise of the back garden.'

At trade union level, there appears to be a failure of the older men to engage the active interests of the recruits. The main contact seems to be often nothing more than collecting regular subscriptions or with claiming accident or sickness benefits. Carter found that on 'a very generous estimate' hardly more than 'one-third of the respondents—those who were members as well as those who were not—had a reasonably clear picture of more than one or two of the functions of trades unions.'[3] Even at the level of easing youngsters

---

[1] Bednarik, op. cit., p. 115.   [2] Ibid., p. 24.
[3] Carter, op. cit., p. 274.

into industry the unions did not seem to be doing very much to help the incoming generation.

Dr Mark Abrams in a survey carried out analysing contemporary British political attitudes paid particular attention to the young voters between the ages of eighteen and twenty-five who would probably be entitled to vote at the next election.[1] By 1964, when that election took place they constituted 13 per cent of the total electorate, 'more than enough to upset past trends in adult voting and thus to settle decisively the outcome of the election.' His findings, unlike Bednarik's and Godfrey Smith's, do not suggest political apathy amongst young people so much as a chronic timidity and mental conformity. For many, it seems, politics exists to nourish material satisfaction rather than moral good. With 45 per cent of the girls and 25 per cent of the age group today already married, it would not be unreasonable to expect them to be placing security and continuing prosperity high on the list of priorities and Dr Abrams' enquiry carried out towards the end of 1959 gave eloquent testimony to this assumption. On the basis of respondents' replies to two questions 'which party do you support or lean towards?', 'it would seem,' he wrote, 'that among these young people potential Conservative voters now outnumber potential Labour voters.'[2] He found that 'no less than 52 per cent of young people today are Conservatives, 43 per cent are Labour supporters, and five per cent Liberals.' There were no less than '35 per cent of all working-class young people . . . ready to identify themselves with the Conservative Party, and only 10 per cent of middle-class young people' were prepared to 'support the Labour Party.'[3]

Dr Abrams, on the basis of these findings, predicts a swing to the right amongst future young voters, and, while no one is entitled to write this kind of attitude off as implying nothing more than political inertia, the fact that 44 per cent of them opted to vote Tory because this was the party that would benefit them most personally certainly adds further confirmation to the belief that the average member of the rising generation is in favour of a quiet, prosperous, peaceful life and has little taste for the more venturesome idealisms of his father's day.

[1] Mark Abrams, 'Why Labour has Lost Elections, Part Four: Young Voters', *Socialist Commentary*, July 1960, pp. 5–12; published by Penguin Books as *Must Labour Lose?*

[2] Ibid.   [3] Ibid.

On most questions young people gave replies very similar to those of their elders; they are equally preoccupied with the maintenance of economic prosperity and equally disposed to see the Conservatives as more likely to provide this. To an even greater extent than their elders they see the Conservative Party as one supported by middle-class people, and they are more ready than their elders to identify with this class. They are highly optimistic about the future, and very satisfied with their jobs.[1]

The existence of that small band of youthful converts to nuclear disarmament is one of the few indications that some of the nation's youth are still deeply concerned with national and international issues. But they are a minority group, composed probably of artists, intellectuals and the bohemian fringe. The vast majority of teenagers seem to be conformists and quietists. 'Interest in politics,' wrote Professor Bernard, reviewing the available evidence, 'is not an integral part of teenage culture.'[2] Middle and upper class youth is apt to be conservative, lower class youth is more inclined to be 'liberal.' But with respect to civil liberties and rights of ethnic minority groups, working class youth on the whole seemed to exhibit the more reactionary attitudes.[3]

It is not an inspiring picture however one considers it. The bulk are content, it seems, almost to the point of insensitivity and selfish indifference. They accept life and enjoy it as it is. There is little zeal for reform. Politically they are comparatively inactive and it cannot be claimed that our schools, colleges and universities are doing very much in a consistent and constructive way to change the situation.

11

It is not possible to try here to summarise in detail all the material regarding young people's behaviour and attitudes presented in this chapter. But it is perhaps worth while pointing out that, not unexpectedly, there seem to be three major conditioning influences in operation.

These are, first, the influence of parents and the local culture; second, the influence of the peer group; and third, the influence of the school and the teachers. We have insufficient data on which we can yet base any general hypotheses. The studies, moreover, from

---

[1] Mark Abrams, *Socialist Commentary*, op. cit. The political pendulum, however, may well have swung over to the left since this passage was written.
[2] Bernard, op. cit., p. 7.   [3] Ibid., pp. 7–8.

which we have drawn are both British and North American; they not only relate to different kinds of societies but also cover a period of time insufficient to register significant social changes. Nevertheless, for what it is worth, there is a considerable degree of agreement in the researches discussed to suggest that not only is the home and the local milieu of considerable importance, but that the influence of the peer group, too, is highly significant in shaping adolescent values. The peer group, the home and the locality, moreover, may be thought of as varying sectors in a continuum which are themselves basically connected with social class and economic status. Their combined influence may be expected to be great enough more or less to over-whelm whatever pressure the school or the teachers may strive to exert in a contrary direction. If Hollingshead is correct, moreover, teachers' attitudes and the very organisation of the schools are themselves deeply ingrained with class bias and to a very considerable extent serve to reinforce the existing *status quo*.[1]

The child is thought of as the more or less passive recipient of social pressures and cultural influences. Growing up is a process in which he is unconsciously 'being moulded into a personality that is simultaneously a creature of his experiences and a creator of new situations in which he will act as a moulder of conduct.'[2] The chances are, therefore, heavily in favour of a conservative outlook. 'By the time he reaches adolescence,' wrote Hollingshead, 'his personality is formed.' He has by this time developed 'conceptions of (1) himself; (2) the social structure; (3) his place in it along with appropriate roles and statuses; (4) forms of behaviour, approved and disapproved; and (5) means of doing what he desires even though it involves the violation of law and the mores.'[3] Hence it is that parents and clique mates, being almost entirely in the same social class, are the most powerful arbiters of taste and conditioners of values and attitudes. Social class stratification acts throughout the process. In Britain, certainly, it would be widely admitted as the most significant aspect of the growing up process, although in the United States, sociologists apart, there might well be some ideolo-gical objections to such a notion. Havighurst and his colleagues seem to believe that 'a good school system teaches boys and girls of different social backgrounds to get along together, and thus build a cohesive society.'[4]

---

[1] Hollingshead, op. cit.   [2] Ibid., p. 445.
[3] Ibid.   [4] Havighurst, *et al.*, op. cit., p. 161.

But since, as they admit, this means following in the parents' footsteps, education remains a mainly conservative force. They would qualify this however by pointing out that, nevertheless, it does enable 'a sizable and important minority of lower-class boys and girls' to prepare for and later to attain 'life in a higher social class than the one they were born into.'[1]

The true test is to what extent youngsters are enabled to develop their talents and rise on the social scale, and, further, to what extent are those born into a more lowly way of life enabled to achieve an adequate standard of living compatible with their dignity as human personalities of equal importance with those more favourably placed. In the final analysis, a civilisation or a society is to be judged not on the quality of life of its outstanding citizens but of the lowest echelons in the social hierarchy. We should not ask what the *modus vivendi* of general and headquarters staff is so much as what life is like for the private soldiers.

No British study adequately supplies answers to these questions but Havighurst's River City enquiry suggests what is happening in the United States and very likely what is going on in British society too. Havighurst divided his research group into six separate categories in his assessment of the degree of success attained by the school system and other community institutions 'in building a cohesive society.'

Groups 1 and 3 are the upward-mobile ones, making up 19 per cent of the age group. They are the ones whose life chances have been enhanced by the schools and other youth-serving agencies. They are the ones to whom River City can point with pride as products of a democratic society that extends opportunity to youth. Groups 2 and 5 are the stable ones, who will lead satisfying and constructive lives at the same social class levels as their parents, either middle class or working class. They make up 52 per cent of the age group. Although the schools might have made a better job with them through stimulating them to more intellectual effort and more artistic activity, they are, nevertheless, the great stabilising force of the next generation.

Groups 4 and 6 are those with whom River City has failed, and there are a dangerous 29 per cent of them. The drifters and the alienated, they have not made use of what the schools offered them, and the community has not been able to offset what in many cases

[1] Havighurst, *et al.*, op. cit., p. 161.

was an inadequate home and in some probably an inferior biological constitution.

They come from all social classes in roughly equivalent proportions, though the lower-middle class seems to furnish more than its proportional share of them. They are the elements making for instability and disunity in the society.[1]

Such an outcome, if generally true, is far from satisfactory and suggests that there is a substantial minority of young people, at least in American society, who are likely to become social misfits and present problems to themselves and to the rest of the community. A failure rate of nearly 30 per cent is surely not good enough for a country which enjoys a rising and exceptionally high standard of living and which believes itself to have discovered the final answer to all man's political problems in his pursuit of the 'good life.' We may do a little better in this country. Our proportion of failures and potential misfits may be rather smaller. Only a similar comprehensive research project could establish this as a fact, and, to date, no such enquiry has been attempted. But even if it could be demonstrated that we are producing a somewhat smaller group of potential outcasts, there is little ground for complacency.

A society like the United States which is essentially directed towards the achievement of personal success and which richly rewards those who have 'got what it takes' and which at the same time downgrades those who fail in such a competitive atmosphere is not necessarily more ruthless or unjust than ours. If in Britain we may expect to find fewer misfits or rejects we could also reasonably expect to find fewer upward-mobiles, to use the sociologist's jargon. Each society very likely has the defects of its virtues. While, in the United States it may well be that ambitiousness serves to intensify frustrations, in Britain the striving for equality and fair play may, in the end, breed mere mediocrity.

Clearly social class and family background are vital determinants of the success or failure of most boys and girls in the long drawn out growing up process. While the vast majority may be said to live through this experience with varying degrees of success, the cost of their adjustment seems unfortunately to involve a perhaps excessive amount of conformity. Well adjusted youngsters are all too like their well adjusted parents and middle class norms seem to be expanding their sphere of influence as the educational process grinds

[1] Havighurst, *et al.*, op. cit., p. 163.

on from generation to generation. The two great social problems, then, that seem to be emerging are (a) what to do to prevent the failures becoming socially alienated and reactive against authority, and (b) how to get the vast body of conformist youth to take a more adventurous and idealistic attitude to the world. The first is the problem of delinquency and juvenile unrest; the other, of dull mediocrity which may in the final analysis prove to be the more widespread attitude and thus present us with the severer social problem.

1

The personal goal of the adolescent is to achieve maturity. At the emotional level this implies an ability to make and to maintain firm relationships with other people. The hallmark of psychological maturity is hence an ability to establish a set of good human relationships. The immature individual is, by definition, socially isolated or else childishly dependent upon other people's ministrations. The mature personality, on the other hand, can, when necessary, stand alone, but nevertheless is usually found to have succeeded in forging strong bonds of loyalty, affection and understanding with at least one or two other persons.

In adolescence the traits developed in childhood do not disappear but are expanded and strengthened. So, too, in early maturity the characteristics of the adolescent which have emerged out of childish habits and reactions are also often discernible. So strong indeed is the impact of the adolescent phase that many people not only retain its imprint on their behaviour and personalities throughout the remainder of their lives, but they seem to be more or less arrested in a permanent adolescent condition. In particular, some Englishmen seem never to outgrow the emotions generated during their public school days but to live forever after bathed in a warm nostalgic glow left behind by the hearty, philistine, spartan life which is no more. It was, I think, the critic Cyril Connolly who directed attention to this odd trait in some upper class English authors, which has been called the 'theory of permanent adolescence.'

Arrested adolescents probably grow out of arrested children. The extreme emphasis on youth in contemporary society perhaps accounts for the legend that most Englishmen anyway are little more than schoolboys for the best part of their lives. That is why, no doubt, they have also acquired the reputation of being somewhat jejune and technically incompetent lovers and, on the other hand, so madly devoted to games and sports.

What happens to an individual during the adolescent stage, therefore, is as important psychologically as what happened during the first five years, although it has not received the same amount of attention in recent research literature. The irrevocability of impressions established during the early years is a dogma that dies hard in psychoanalytical circles. But it is on the wane and a more realistic appraisal of the significance of every developmental phase is coming to be accepted. Unlike childhood or infancy 'adolescence is a much more social or even socio-economic phenomenon than it is a biological one.'[1] Hence, it is the psycho-social tensions and interactions which are of supreme importance at this time. The main difference between the child and the adolescent is that the latter has attained physiological sexual maturity. This is what the psychoanalyst means when he speaks of adolescence 'as a terminal stage of the fourth phase of psychosexual development, the genital phase, which' during the preceding few years has 'been interrupted by the latency period.'[2]

The boy or girl of fifteen or sixteen is capable of sexual intercourse and usually of procreation. It is the social and traditional forces of our civilisation which produce a state of affairs in which this is the exception rather than the rule. Many of our moral problems arise precisely because physiological and social maturity do not coincide in our culture. There is a vigorous sex drive apparent in both sexes at adolescence which, to quote Dr Wall once again, 'at least in the early stages, reinforces aggressiveness and accounts in some measure for the unruliness, difficult behaviour and even delinquency which is a marked feature of the period between 12 and 15.'[3]

The psychoanalyst would put it in somewhat different terms but suggest the same thing. To the analysts adolescence is a kind of second childhood for what both periods have in common is 'the fact that a "relatively strong id confronts a relatively weak ego" (A. Freud, 1936)'[4] at that time—a condition that makes for extreme vulnerability.

The emergence of primary and secondary sexuality is therefore one of the few hard facts we know about the teenager. A related fact is that our society, like most others, does not approve of sexual behaviour under the age of, at least, eighteen, and there is, as a consequence, an awkward interim stage between the manifestation

[1] Wall, *Education and Mental Health*, op. cit., p. 135.

[2] P. Blos, *On Adolescence, A Psychoanalytical Interpretation*; Free Press, 1962, p. 1.

[3] Wall, *Education and Mental Health*, op. cit., p. 138.

[4] Blos, op. cit., p. 11. The quotation from Anna Freud comes from her book, *The Ego and the Mechanisms of Defence*.

of sexuality and its socially permitted expression. Things can go wrong during this interim stage quite dramatically as when a proportion of young girls become pregnant. They can also go wrong, much less obviously and with equally far-reaching consequences, for a possibly greater number of youngsters whose sexual expression is turned inwards on themselves in auto-eroticism, or whose urges are bottled up and released through violent substitute outlets or those others who direct their physical and emotional interests towards members of their own sex as being the only available or convenient love objects in their environment. At the same time it is only fair to say that, as far as can be judged by subsequent behaviour, a great many youngsters manage to live through this awkward interim period without breaking out in forbidden or undesirable forms of expression and without suffering psychological injury. They may find permitted outlets in exhibitionist athleticism or romantic aestheticism. They may flirt gently with members of their own sex without going to the lengths of having any proscribed physical exchanges. They may also begin to flirt with members of the opposite sex without indulging in 'heavy petting' or more serious involvement. They seem to find their way between the rapids and the rocks and out into the open sea of adulthood without being swamped, stranded or wrecked. A great and unknown number do. We must not forget about them, or become so obsessed with those who manifest difficulty that youth is never seen in our culture as anything else than a grave social and psychological problem.

Above all we must not be stampeded either by the Freudian and neo-freudian psychoanalysts, or by the young Goslings on the other hand, into a wholesale withdrawal from commitment and responsibility. Parents and teachers, youth leaders and others charged with the task of assisting youngsters to grow up must not weakly abdicate in the face of criticism or abandon their posts because difficulties arise.

They need to be aware of their own fears and of their reluctance to let youngsters grow into autonomy. Change does not always spell disharmony however. Growing up need not mean a fundamental growing away.

2

There seem to me to be two fairly widespread fallacies about how we ought and ought not to bring up young people nowadays. The first springs mainly from the psychoanalytical view that we must always accept adolescence on its own terms. In a recent article, for example, Dr D. W. Winnicott summarised this approach when he claimed that the behaviour of even 'the normal adolescent is related to that which shows in various kinds of ill persons.'[1] He compares the schizophrenic's inability to compromise with a youth's healthy repudiation of any false solution or easy compromise, and the psychoneurotic's ambivalence with ordinary people's tendencies to deceive themselves. Dr Winnicott may or may not be right in relating these instances of apparently normal and abnormal behaviour as representing different points on a conduct continuum, but he is surely going beyond the evidence when he deduces that 'from this it follows that in a group of adolescents the various tendencies tend to be represented by the more ill members of the group. One member of a group takes an overdose of a drug, another lies in bed in a depression, another is free with the flick knife. In each case there are grouped a band of adolescent isolates behind the ill individual whose extreme symptom has impinged on society.'[2]

The sick individual who gets depressed, who is quick on the draw, who swallows too many sleeping pills, represents similar but weaker urges in a host of others for whom he acts vicariously. As Dr Winnocott puts it, 'the ill one had to act for the others.'

So, too, on the basis of this argument the young delinquent expresses the juvenile reaction to a fundamental emotional deprivation from which all youngsters to varying degrees suffer. Delinquency is hence a 'type of illness.'

In the root of the antisocial tendency is deprivation. In the root of healthy adolescence in general it is not possible to say that there is inherently a deprivation, but still there is something in a diffused way which is the same but in a degree not strong enough to overstrain the available defences. This means that in the group that the adolescent finds to identify with, the extreme members of the group are acting for the total group.[3]

If I follow this argument correctly, 'illness' is to be understood as a result of deprivation which itself results from the experience of frustration. Youth in particular is a time of general frustration,

[1] D. W. Winnicott, 'Struggling Through The Doldrums', *New Society*, No. 30, 1963, pp. 8–11.
[2] Ibid.   [3] Ibid.

hence serious deprivations may have to be endured during these years and consequently the pathogenic risks are greatly increased. Delinquency, excessive retreatism, drug addiction, violence and aggression are all symptoms of psychological illness or un-health. Not many adolescents will give way to such extreme outbursts but most will be in sympathy with these impulsive urges. The rebel represents the majority. Adolescence is hence, on the basis of this line of analysis, itself a kind of social illness. The need to defy and challenge which some adolescents seem to possess to an inordinate degree is symptomatic of the fundamental malaise of this phase of their development. We must expect this kind of thing to happen and be ready for it in every generation, realising that the reactive nonconformist minority are not outsiders from youth culture but actually represent and express the generally experienced social and psychological maladjustment which is the inevitable concomitant of that stage. Dr Winnocott calls this the 'adolescent doldrums' and urges us to think of this awkward and semi-sick period of the life span 'as a permanent feature and to tolerate it, to go to meet it, but not to cure it.' The attitude of adults must be based on fundamental sympathetic support and understanding, coupled with the realisation that there is little or nothing that they can do in a positive way to help at this critical stage. The only hope of cure is time. One day or the other day, the aggressive, irrascible and turbulent youth will sober down into a more or less willing recruit to the social world of his parents. He will emerge from the doldrums, hoist his own sails and join the fleet. We hope!

The general view outlined in the preceding paragraph may be held to be representative of many psychologists and psychiatrists. It clearly has much to commend it and advances a number of hypotheses which seem to fit some of the available evidence.

In particular it does account very well for the conspicuous protest element in adolescent behaviour which has been so widely observed and adversely commented upon. Its main weakness is its explicit determinism, the suggestion that things cannot be altered and that, as a society, we have no alternative to accepting 'adolescent doldrums' in some degree as a permanent social phenomenon. I will put the objections to this position in a later chapter. For the moment it is sufficient to note that the idea of inevitability of conflict is closely associated with the notion of a necessary element of illness involved in the adolescent phase.

3

The concept of adolescence as an almost sick developmental stage
is in accord with another widely held psychological and psychiatric
idea which is frequently advanced today, that of the 'sick society.'
The whole of modern society, we are told, is diseased. It is not merely
that there are pathogenic factors at work in social relations and
social affairs but the entire social structure is in some way ill. In a
recent report on the deliberations of a group of experts convened at
the U.N.E.S.C.O. Youth Institute near Munich, this concept is stated
as a more or less self-evident truth.

Perhaps comparison is impossible, but some people have the feeling
that the situation as a whole is today very much more difficult and serious
than it was formerly, for on the one hand society, or rather the social
sphere in which the individual grows up, is sick; on the other, the majority
of individuals are sick. This is shown, for example, in the fact that many
children in school are to a large degree repressed and neurotic—on the
average, ten to fifteen per cent of those in each class—so that a normal
teacher can no longer cope because so many children need special treatment. It often seems that we are not sufficiently aware of the sort of
volcano on which we are sitting. But if, for example, the economic bottom
in most of our countries should collapse, and a struggle for jobs, and for
life itself, should develop, these difficulties would become apparent on an
alarming scale.[1]

Now if this diagnosis is well-founded then we are indeed in a
parlous condition. If Society is sick and most individuals are mentally ill the future of our civilisation is clearly imperilled. It is not an
idea we should dismiss out of hand as altogether inconceivable. The
atrocities perpetrated in the Nazi extermination camps, the brutal
bombing of Dresden by the R.A.F. and the dropping of two atom
bombs on Japan during the Second World War indicate the kind
of moral abyss which can suddenly open beneath our feet. But
before we can give credence to the concept of the sick society we are
entitled to ask for the evidence and to expect that the evidence will
be of such a kind that it can be examined and measured against past
conditions.

Unfortunately the sole basis for the idea of the sick society resides
in the fallible statistics of ascertained mental illness which are
everywhere said to be on the increase. However, as we do not

[1] *School and Social Maladjustment of Youth*, Report of a meeting of Experts,
Institut der Jugend, Gauting/München, April, 1960, p. 8.

possess anything like accurate or utilisable records of the past and since the definitions of mental illnesses are neither explicit nor objectively defined, nor static nor universally agreed, very little of a substantial nature can be construed from such figures as we possess. All that the increasing incidence of known mental illness seems to indicate is a growing diagnostic sensitivity and subtlety on the one hand and a more widespread desire for treatment on the other. On the evidence available, the case for the sick society must be dismissed as not proven. All the same we should as a community be alert to the possibility that mental ill health is multiplying and scrutinise our social institutions to see whether or not they might be fostering psychopathic tendencies. Further than this it would be most unwise to go. Sociologists, above all, are not likely to be greatly impressed by the new 'mental healthmanship' approach which, in the last few years, has increasingly striven to put every 'undesirable' form of human behaviour down to some kind of illness or personal mal-functioning. The notion that adolescence is a sort of social illness or similarly that juvenile delinquency is often due to mental disturb-ance and is only to be expected in the circumstances and can only be treated by medical doctors, not only offends against common sense, it also undermines the whole basis of established law and order.

As Barbara Wootton wrote in a now famous text, 'psychiatrists since Freud have been busy doing for man's morals what Darwin and Huxley did for his pedigree, and with not much less success.'[1]

We cannot, in good conscience, leave it to the medical or psychia-tric experts to get us all well again and so cure the general social malaise. If there is a 'Youth Problem' (and there seems to be some evidence to suggest that some young people are behaving problem-atically) then we have a democratic duty to examine this responsibly together in the light of reason and morality and see what we should do about it.

4

While we may be far from being convinced that adolescence is by nature a sick phase, we may yet accept the idea than an element of turbulence is a not too unlikely characteristic at this time of life nor

[1] Barbara Wootton, *Social Science and Social Pathology*, Allen and Unwin, 1959, p. 398.

necessarily a bad prognosis for future development. We acknowledge that the changes brought about by pubescence are crucial and dramatic and that they may, temporarily at least, lead to an apparent clash of values between the generations with consequent disciplinary and parental problems. It is clear that a situation in which maturing sexuality goes hand in hand with continued economic, social and legal dependence contains within itself powerful potentialities for rebellion and strife.

Some degree of rebellion may be necessary and desirable but too much may precipitate the condition of social malaise to which Dr Winnicott and others have directed our attention. Edgar Friedenberg in his penetrating analysis of adolescence in contemporary American society has especially deplored the falling off in rebelliousness in most youthful behaviour.[1] 'It is the fully human adolescent—the adolescent who faces life with love and defiance—who has become aberrant. Real adolescents are vanishing', and their place is being taken, so Friedenberg argues, by pale conformists busily imitating grown-up attitudes.

Maturing sexuality is undoubtedly one if not the most potent complicating factor at this stage but surely it need not be supposed to lead to inevitable illness? That it does so, from time to time, is not denied. That it need necessarily do so is questioned. Coming to terms with one's own expanding sexuality is a basic human problem. It is one which the teenager experiences with unique difficulty for not only is he sexually and in other ways a comparative tyro, but furthermore it is generally believed that the sheer pressure for physical release attains its maximum strength in the late adolescent years. Ernest A. Smith in a discussion of the relevant American literature on the subject indicated that the onset of full functional potency is an especially acute problem for the male.

An average male frequency is about 3·4 releases a week, the peak occurring from about seventeen to twenty years of age (Kinsey, Pomeroy and Martin, 1948, p. 219). Lower-class boys of high school level are 20 to 30 per cent more active than college-level males (Kinsey, Pomeroy and Martin, 1948, p. 335). This adolescent peak highlights the discontinuity in formal structure; the law and mores approve outlet only in marriage, yet unmarried boys are more sexually active than even young married men.[2]

[1] Friedenberg, op. cit., p. 18.

[2] Ernest A. Smith, *American Youth Culture*; The Free Press, Macmillan, New York, 1962, pp. 129–30. The book referred to in the quotation is *Sexual Behaviour in the Human Male*; Saunders, 1948.

Girls, by contrast, are said to have only a 'fraction of the sexual activity of the adolescent boy. By fifteen years of age 92 per cent of the males experience orgasm, as against 25 per cent of the girls.'[1]

Whether the evidence on the famous Kinsey investigation can be taken to be universally true is still an open question. But even if we make some allowance for the fact that the sort of people who are not disinclined to discuss the facts of their sex life openly with a third party are not truly representative of the population and may to some degree be aroused more easily and have been chronologically earlier in their development, the basic problem remains unaltered.

If we add a twelve-month to Kinsey's estimate of the age by which the vast majority of males achieve their first orgasm, we are still confronted by the probability that older schoolboys or those in their first year at work are already sexually active in the physiological sense.

It has further been argued that what holds true for North America need not be taken as gospel for European countries and that in Britain, especially, sexual activity is usually delayed rather longer. However, even if we accept this unsupported argument it is reasonable to suppose that British boys for the most part nowadays have a sex life long before the usual age of marriage is reached.

Since the sheer physical pressures are strongest on males, it will be clear that *vis-à-vis* females they are somewhat disadvantaged. On the whole they marry at a later date. One of the most dramatic social changes that have occurred in recent years is the lowering of the average age of marriage. The commonest age for marriage in Britain is now 22 for men and 21 for women as compared with an average of 25 and 23 a decade ago.[2] The fact that there are now a great many teenage marriages suggests that young people find it harder than hitherto to wait for legal majority before embarking on matrimony. The trend for earlier marriages may well continue and we may possibly witness a still further reduction in the average age of wedlock by the end of the present century.

The sheer logic of these hard facts may well bring about a radical reappraisal of our general attitude to youth. On the other hand,

[1] Ernest A. Smith, *American Youth Culture*; The Free Press, 1962, pp. 129–30.
[2] In the U.S.A. the average marriage age for men is rather higher (24) and for girls it is about the same as in Britain. See Smith, op. cit., p. 209.

strong resistance is to be expected from some moralists against any such tendency which they may interpret as a mere giving way to youthful irresponsibility.

5

Two factors which are generally held to be responsible for the greater popularity of marriage today and for the lowering of the age of matrimony are young people's growing economic independence and an accelerated rate of physical maturation. In an earlier section we have already discussed the rising tide of teenage affluence and some of its social consequences. Probably the most important result of this financial self-sufficiency is the ability to marry and set up home, and, provided that the standard of living continues at more or less its present level, this is likely to exert a steady pressure in the same direction for many years ahead.

Earlier physical maturation is a much more questionable influence. In the first place the evidence for an earlier average age for the onset of puberty is far from being unequivocal. Dr J. M. Tanner has examined the relevant data in some detail and he has concluded that there is a secular trend over the last hundred years or so for the time of puberty to come earlier.[1] Statistics of height and weight show that children of all socio-economic groups born in the nineteen-thirties were larger than those born thirty years previously.

Trends in Sweden and America were apparently similar to those in this country. Swedish figures kept between 1880 and 1950 suggest that there has been an average gain per decade of some two centimetres and one and a half kilogrammes. It is claimed that whereas maximum height used to be reached at the age of twenty-six, boys in the higher social classes in Europe and the U.S.A. attain it somewhere between their eighteenth and nineteenth birthdays and girls between the ages of sixteen and seventeen. Members of the high income groups are everywhere said to be more advanced in their growth. In Sweden there seems to be correlation between height and social class and high bodily weight is shown to be associated with intellectual ability and the obtaining of a grammar school type education.

Information about the age for the onset of menarche for girls is extremely sketchy for Great Britain but rather better for Scandinavia.

[1] J. M. Tanner, *Growth at Adolescence*; Blackwell, 1955.

Figures quoted for the United States are based on one women's college only, which may or may not be representative of the country as a whole. All the figures so far available seem to point to the fact that the age of maturation is getting earlier and earlier, by about a third to a half year per decade between 1850 and 1950. In a century, therefore, the average age of maturity is thought to have fallen from seventeen to thirteen years, and if this is so there is no apparent reason why it should not fall even lower in the future. Most recent data give the average age of menarche of white Americans as somewhere between twelve and a half and thirteen according to social class. In schools in the south of England in 1950 the average of thirteen and a half was noted, likewise in Western Germany.

Biologists are particularly interested in this phenomenon and account for it mainly in terms of better nutrition and improved health services. Knowledge of vitamins and their relation to growth and general vitality may have assisted the process together with a better physical environment in most places, but it is doubtful whether the lower income groups, who might have been excessively retarded in less equalitarian days, have revealed a more pronounced growth spurt than the children of better off parents.

It is extremely important in all discussion concerning the age by which youngsters achieve full sexual maturity to realise that there is immense variation between individuals and that individuals themselves progress more often by fits and starts than by a continuous growth. We must also remember that the criteria of maturity are somewhat arbitrary and that the appearance of menstruation in girls does not necessarily mean that they have the ability to conceive and bear children.[1]

Another caveat concerns the popular idea that girls mature physically earlier than boys. As Dr Fleming has shown from an examination of the relevant data 'this assumption is not supported by the evidence from long-term studies of adolescent development.' The average difference between the two sexes is probably not more than six months. Furthermore, if other criteria are used, 'such as the appearance of pigmented and curly pubic hair in the case of boys there seems reason to believe that girls and boys reach com-

---

[1] Cf. Blos, op. cit., p. 8. 'Menarche is usually considered the sign that the girl has achieved sexual maturity. In fact this event really signals that the maturation of the reproductive organs is under way but is by no means complete.'

parable stages of sexual development at approximately the same ages.'[1]

Another point of interest and frequent conjecture is whether or not this secular trend in growth rates alleged to have taken place in western societies during the past hundred years or so represents a new rhythm or whether it is in fact a return to an older and temporarily disturbed growth rate. Alex Comfort takes the view that it has happened not as the outcome of a radical biological change but is 'the restoration of a more normal developmental timing which something at the beginning of the nineteenth century had greatly slowed down.'[2] In Roman times, for example, girls were assumed to be marriageable at the age of twelve plus. Speculation centres around the intense urban poverty and squalid living conditions which characterised the Industrial Revolution as a possible braking influence, though why this should have happened it is hard to see, at the same time, there was a phenomenal bulge in the birth rate and the population of these islands went up by leaps and bounds.

The whole topic is shrouded in mystery. Evidence is not only thin, it is sometimes dubious. It is difficult to be sure exactly how puberty is to be gauged in boys as not all secondary sexual characteristics appear simultaneously and there can really never be any way of knowing when an individual experiences his first seminal flow. With girls more precision is possible as the first menstruation is something that is hardly likely to be forgotten. But, bearing in mind the extreme prudery of Victorian society, it is difficult to believe that such things would in the past be discussed or answered accurately enough to satisfy the canons of a truly scientific enquiry.

Altogether, in the face of the conflicting views and extremely sketchy and partial evidence available, we should treat the claim for earlier physiological maturation with caution. Even if it were in the future to be proved beyond any reasonable doubt, we need not credit it with the greatest influence in promoting earlier marriage.

Other and, to my mind, more significant forces are at work. There is, I believe, something we may term social maturity, compounded of physical preparedness, psychological expectation and motivation and economic autonomy which is almost irresistibly compelling young people not only into marriage but into earlier and earlier matrimony. Ideas and influences abroad in the climate of the

---

1 Fleming, op. cit., p. 156.
2 Alex Comfort, 'Growing Up Faster'; *The Listener*, July 7, 1960, pp. 15–16.

times exert an inexorable pressure in the direction of conformity at the sexual or rather at the psycho-socio-sexual level. Girls know that the main rewards and satisfactions of their lives are still intimately bound up with marriage and family life. For the majority it is still the only career open to them; it is the surest way for the less gifted or less enterprising and even for the average girl to achieve social status.

An engagement ring is a highly esteemed status symbol. A career for the majority still seems to offer a somewhat barren and unromantic future, unless perhaps it lies in the field of medicine. Earlier maturity and early social pressure send the girls quickly out into the marriage market in search of their future husbands. Both imitation and competition are operative in the situation. For working class girls this comprises the major business of their whole lives. Middle class girls tend to approach the problem rather later but even they know that if they pass the age of thirty without attachment their chances of matrimony grow less and less. For it is still customary in our culture, especially amongst 'respectable' families and in their related social circle, for the males to be the initiators. 'Nice' girls cannot make the first approach to the youth of their choice or interest. They can be ready in response but still must await the invitation to go out with a male to a dance or to a concert. They may be ever so subtle and inventive in liming their snares but the men must take the initial step of walking into the trap. It is far easier for an older man to get married than it is for an older woman. All along the line, in respectable society, initiative rests with the males, but even they nowadays tend to be on the look out for a mate somewhat earlier and more eagerly than heretofore. The balance of the sexes has shifted of recent years so that now, in place of a former surplus of women, there is an excess of men.

Bachelors are likely to be much more common than spinsters in the years ahead. In the past the devoted army of teachers, social workers and nurses society needed were in the main recruited from the ranks of supernumerary unmarried women whose numbers are rapidly running out. It is quite clear that if we are to replace them in the future many more married women than at present will be required to do part-time and even full-time work to make good the deficiency.

The fact that unattached girls are becoming in even shorter supply is probably making boys more competitive in seeking to attract their attention and to win their favours. This may well be one aspect of the growing dandyism observable in post-war young males. Their greater clothes consciousness and desire for self-display could in many instances be associated with a more competitive courtship. In the Edwardian era men were similarly fashion conscious and at still earlier times set out to attract attention with every sartorial and other device at their disposal. The age of 'dowdiness' is over, apart from the deliberate rejection of colour by the beatnik fringe groups, the habitual slovenliness of the over-fifties and the insouciant dirtiness of some undergraduates. We would do well to glory in the passing of a grey epoch in the nation's history and welcome every fresh advent of colour and style ushered in by the rising generation as a positive aesthetic and social gain.[1]

6

The increasing popularity of marriage is one of the most surprising demographic facts of recent years.[2] The period from the age of ten to twenty may be regarded as partly a preparation for matrimony, and partly a temporary retreat from the threatened responsibility. The age-homogeneous or, as they are often called, peer, groups which we referred to in previous chapters were seen to have grown up to meet these two specific and dichotomous youthful needs. North American society has witnessed in recent years the birth of a patterned youth culture which, although an indigenous and spontaneous reaction to a general situation, is almost certainly germane to our own cultural needs. Teenage social institutions in Britain have not as yet been made the target for detailed investigation but when they are explored it is more than likely that similar if not identical institutions will be identified. In Canada and the U.S.A. an entirely new practice, the 'date,' has come into being to function as a 'major transitional institution of youth culture,'[3] outstandingly adopted by middle class and college trained young people. In Britain, although youngsters have imitated the expression and speak

[1] I am not unaware that these manifestations of increasing self-adornment on the part of males can equally derive to some extent from a delayed or rather prolonged narcissism and even, in individual instances, from a positively homosexual base.

[2] Even in Tudor times when the expectation of life was considerably less than it is today marriage under twenty was apparently uncommon.

[3] Smith, op. cit., p. 147.

loosely of 'dating a girl', the term here has not yet attained the full institutionalised force that it has in America. 'A most interesting aspect of the date,' says Ernest A. Smith, 'is that, of all youth institutions, it varies most from adult norms.'[1]

The date is a social rather than a personal concept. It permits youngsters to consort together, to have limited physical relations, but does not in any way bind them together in a stable or exclusive union. Popular youths can have several dates going on more or less simultaneously without giving cause for jealousy. 'Romantic love,' says Smith, 'is least relevant during dating, although it simulates romantic love by using its language devoid of "meaning".'[2] This device gives young people the opportunity to orient themselves heterosexually, to have limited but 'aim-inhibited' sexual experience at a time when, for social, economic and cultural reasons, complete adult status is denied. In so far as heterosexuality is matured during the dating phase the practice may be said to be forward looking, but, if carried on too far and too long, it may ultimately prove dysfunctional for the later married state. During adolescence boys and girls hive off in couples to indulge in, free from parental scrutiny, what has come to be called 'petting'. Petting is a word coming more and more into vogue but I can myself remember it being used in my own schooldays in the nineteen-thirties when some of my contemporaries indulged in what they called 'petting parties' which I occasionally attended as a fringe figure. At these parties couples retired to secluded nooks to indulge in mutual physical exploration. The leading spirits led the way and tried to persuade the more reluctant and guilt-laden fringe group to follow suit, but, as is frequently observed at dances, a proportion of the lads preferred to observe from a safe distance. Petting can, of course, consist of little more than the kisses and cuddles of good old Edwardian days, nowadays referred to more often as 'necking'. But 'heavy petting' can go much further and reach the pitch of orgasm. As Smith has indicated, 'date-courtship norms are largely incompatible with the married state. The more successful youth are in the date-courtship role, the less prepared they are for marital adjustment'.[3] This is especially true for the girls whose role in petting may frequently be to fend off the boys' more demanding sexual advances without at the same time causing them to lose interest. The feminine role is therefore a particularly tricky one, consisting of limited giving and

---

[1] Smith, op. cit., p. 147.   [2] Ibid., pp. 147–8.   [3] Ibid., p. 212.

ingenious preventive tactics, and this delicate equilibrium of court-ezanly enticement and maidenly virginity may in the end develop an attitude inimical to the full self-giving required in matrimony. Or, to quote Smith once again, 'the conflict between petting and full surrender in marriage, particularly for women, may be met by emotional revulsion and refusal.'[1] Serious psycho-sexual mal-adjustment may result from this emotional conflict which, in a society as easy-going as the United States, can contribute powerfully to a generous divorce rate on the grounds of mutual incompati-bility.

Dating and subsequent petting sessions are part and parcel of the gay round of parties and dances and sorority meetings which constitute the 'good time' which most young people are eager to pursue while they may, and, like most alluring rosebuds, they are not unattended by punitive thorns. But certain risks seem to be well worth the taking and, as Seeley said about the Canadian upper class community he and his colleagues studied in depth some few years ago, 'for a few years they may escape without guilt into sheer irresponsibility and high spirits, enjoying each other . . . as human beings, exchanging intimacies, having crushes, trying out hetero-sexual relationships, learning the social ropes.'[2] But the golden age cannot be permitted to last for long. Soon the inexorable standards of adult life begin to make inroads into adolescent society. Children are called away from the regressive security of the peer group, fraternity and sorority, which cover the pubescent period, and via dating begin by the age of sixteen to eighteen to conform to what is deemed to be appropriate quasi-adult behaviour.

Adolescence is hence a period of trial and potential tribulation. Parents watch anxiously from the side lines as the various crises arise and fresh squalls blow up. They may resent the fact that their children seem to be leaving them and prefer the company of their age-mates to their parents. They may also, as some psychiatrists have suggested, be more than a little jealous of their children's apparent freedom from responsibility and of their opportunities for experimentation. Most, I think, who love their children dis-interestedly and compassionately are not motivated by either jealousy of undue possessiveness. But they are concerned, and rightly so, knowing the dangers and pitfalls that surround youngsters at this stage of their growth. While it argues mere panic to become

[1] Smith, op. cit., p. 213.   [2] Seeley, et al., op. cit., p. 335.

obsessed with these dangerous possibilities, we cannot entirely ignore them or merely dismiss them as unfounded.

What are the disconcerting facts which make so many parents anxious for their adolescent children? First and perhaps foremost is the rate of illegitimate births in relation to the ages of the un-married mothers. Just as the age of marriage has dropped, so has the age of the girls who conceive out of wedlock. But the proportion of girls who do so remains comparatively low. The age of the mother was not recorded until 1938 and we cannot therefore usefully compare pre-war generations. However, there is a trend in the direction of increasing illegitimacy.

In 1949, of every 10,000 girls age 14 to 20, 37 had illegitimate babies. By 1956 the figure was 45; by 1958, 49. Conceptions at 12–17 were 30 in 10,000 in 1949: 38 in 1956; 42 in 1958. As for shot-gun marriages, of all girls getting married at 20 or under, 29 per cent in 1958 were pregnant at the time. Some 52 per cent of all babies born to girls of 20 or under were conceived out of wedlock. The equivalent figures for 1948 were 30 and 55.[1]

The proportion of teenage brides already pregnant upon marriage has hence remained fairly steady in the past decade, and indeed for a longer period. As long ago as 1939 the Registrar-General's figures showed that no less than 27 per cent of youthful brides were in that year in the same condition upon their wedding day.

It is also a fact that teenage marriages have nowadays a fair chance of ending in divorce. One in five indeed did in the nineteen-fifties, but as there are no earlier statistics available to compare these with we cannot yet regard this as exceptional. The chances of teenage marriages ending in divorce or separation, are, however, propor-tionately greater than for those in their early twenties, thus suggesting that an element of immaturity or sheer ignorance may have led some of the young people into wedlock with a partner for whom they soon acquired a positive aversion. Not unnaturally, the younger the brides and grooms the more hazardous the undertaking seems to be. But this does not mean that teenage marriage *ipso facto* is un-desirable or bound to fail. The vast majority of youthful couples do indeed succeed in sticking it out with apparent success or, at least, commendable fortitude.

[1] Stuart Maclure, 'Teenage Morals in an Age of Uncertainty', in *Teenage Morals*, Councils and Education Press, 1961, p. 6.

A second cause for alarm is to be found in the increasing numbers of cases of unlawful sexual intercourse with girls under thirteen years of age and similarly where the girl is under sixteen. What we do not know is how far girls between the ages of thirteen and sixteen positively connived at illegal intercourse or provoked the offence by some flagrant flirtatiousness. Nor do we know, for that matter, how many of these cases were committed by teenage males or how many by older men.

Finally there is the vexed question of the alleged increased incidence of venereal disease. Gonorrhoea is apparently much more common than it was and is said in some circles to be getting beyond medical control. In spite of the new penicillin treatment it is widespread and increasing in Britain as in most other parts of the world. In the United States there are estimated to be no less than 50,000 youngsters infected annually. The increase was most marked in the 18 to 19 age group but actually seems to have decreased for the 15 to 17 section of the youthful population. Figures are, of course, based on clinical records and there is a possibility that greater willingness to notify infection may account for part of the increase.

It is impossible, however, to deny that gonorrhoea and other venereal infections are presenting serious problems not only in quarters traditionally associated with such ailments such as seaports and garrison towns but in circles which one had imagined to be more immune. For example, Dr R. D. Cattarall of Leeds General Infirmary reporting to a conference on the sex life of university students, subsequently published in the *British Medical Journal*, stated that in the two year period from January 1, 1959, to December 31, 1960, ninety-eight students were treated in the venereal disease clinic. Eighty-eight of this total were males in the 18 to 25 age group, while the women students were mainly between 17 and 20.[1] At the same conference Dr S. E. Finlay of Leeds University reported that twenty-seven unmarried students became pregnant between 1956 and 1960 inclusively, 'an incidence of 1·4 per cent of the total students at risk.'[2] Such partial and not very reliable statistics hint at the growing instability amongst sections of the population enjoying what may be presumed to be favourable environmental conditions and we are probably entitled to suspect that those living in less favourable circumstances are in greater danger.

[1] *The Guardian*, 10/8/62.   [2] Ibid.

On the other hand, there is no reason to regard adolescents as either excessively vulnerable to all forms of sexual irregularities or as atypical of the general culture. Says Ira L. Reiss, Associate Professor of Sociology and Anthropology at the State University of Iowa, 'Teen-age sexual codes reflect quite clearly the bald outlines of adult sexual codes.'[1]

Reiss argues that 'research evidence on sexual codes seem somewhat at odds with the popular view that teenagers have a type of youth culture which in its irresponsibility, extremism, and defiance, is in sharp conflict with adult culture. The venereal disease rates, unwed motherhood rates, and studies of teen-age attitudes give evidence of a more conservative pattern than exists for older couples. The most popular teen-age sexual codes are the double standard for boys and a petting-with-affection code for girls. Another code, which is minor and is strongest among older teenagers, is permissiveness-with-affection, which allows coitus if there is a stable relation present. The custom of "going steady" is closely related to these codes because our culture looks much more favourably upon sexual behaviour when it occurs in such a stable, affectionate context as "going steady" affords.'[2]

Reiss points out, in the same article, that 'the teen-age rate of venereal disease for ages fifteen to nineteen is only about a third of the rate for the twenty to twenty-four age group and is also lower than that of the twenty-five to twenty-nine age group.'[3] Moreover, he says, 'When we compare teen-age unwed motherhood with that for girls in their twenties, we find that the older girls have about the same proportion of the illegitimate children. We also find that the teen-age rates are not increasing as much as the rates for the older groups. For example, in 1940 teen-age unwed mothers were 46 per cent of the total; in 1957 they were forty per cent.'[4]

Andrew McKenzie of Durham University also recently drew our attention to the fact that British figures, contrary to popular stereotyped belief, also indicate a similar state of affairs.

An analysis of figures given in the Registrar-General's Statistical Review shows that a teenage girl has a smaller chance of bearing an illegitimate baby than has any other unmarried woman of childbearing

---

[1] 'Sexual Codes in Teen-age Culture', *Annals* of the American Academy of Political and Social Science, November, 1961, p. 54.
[2] Ibid., p. 53.   [3] Ibid., p. 60.   [4] Ibid., p. 61.

age. The risk is about five times as great for an unmarried woman of 25–35.[1]

The picture, then, when duly adjusted and with gratuitous distortions ironed out, does not justify, even in America, where youngsters may have gone farther in the way of freedom than our own youngsters have, any suggestion of a moral landslide. The generation as a whole is no more likely to break the code governing sexual behaviour than other sections of the population which receive much less publicity. 'They are not as wild as their parents or they themselves sometimes think.'[2] If they strive for autonomy it is nearly always within the framework of existing moral codes. The double standard which males have traditionally enjoyed in western society for such a long time is perhaps a trifle weaker but by no means outmoded. Young men, like their fathers and grandfathers, still seek to lead their girl friends on as far as they can go but, paradoxically, at the same time expect that the girls they will marry and share their adult lives with shall be both chaste and virginal. Marriage is still thought of as a comparatively stable partnership conducted under the benign aura of romantic love. Teenagers are indeed more like ourselves than some of us care to admit. Their shortcomings are largely our own and in their weaknesses and temptations and fallings from grace are mirrored our own failures to live up to the ideals of monogamy and Christian marriage.

7

At the physiological level it is obvious that for some youngsters the tension between rising sexuality and the taboo on overt expression can generate serious difficulties. Adult social norms do not assist young people to accept this state of affairs with equanimity. 'A major discontinuity in the United States,' wrote Smith, 'is found between the emphasis on a "sexless" child and a sexually potent marital role.'[3] He also pointed out that 'the romantic love obsession, combined with the taboo on premarital experience, overvalues the goal of sexual satisfaction in marriage' itself.[4] If the general culture emphasises the ideal of sexual potency and experience, it is almost inevitable that young people will accept it uncritically and that any

---

1 Letter to *The Observer*, 10/3/63.
2 'Sexual Codes in Teen-age Culture', op. cit., p. 67.
3 Smith, op. cit., p. 143.   4 Ibid., p. 212.

failure to achieve romantic sexual satisfaction or any deviancy from the norm will generate anxiety and probably precipitate rash experimentation.

In saying this we are not saying that youth is more likely to behave more unwisely or less moderately than any other age group. We are merely stating the general problem with which all in our culture are faced, but which those on the threshold of adulthood must feel most acutely because of the very nature of their marginal position.

The possible reactions to this state of cultural discontinuity and potential tension may be listed as follows:

(a) strong self-control
(b) sublimation
(c) overt forbidden expression
(d) covert forbidden or condemned expression
(e) the development of new form of institutionalised behaviour appropriate to the youthful condition
(f) earlier marriage

We have already discussed the penultimate possibility and seen how in the United States of America such a solution has been evolved by the predominantly middle class youngsters still in full time attendance at high school or college. The growth of 'the heterosexual crowd' both controls and initiates sexual relationships to such an extent that 'lack of clique experience eliminates this essential training and is very likely to lead to adult maladjustment.'[1]

Lower class youth tend to marry earlier and/or indulge in extra-marital physical relationships with consequent personal and social problems in the way of illegitimacy and young unmarried motherhood.

Neither of these solutions can be said to be ideal.

In Britain it is probable that working class boys and girls behave very similarly to their American counterparts, but that, as far as grammar school and college and university students go, the position is much less institutionalised. No studies have yet been carried out on an extensive scale concerning the sexual outlets which middle class British boys and girls make use of but it is more than probable that they also tend to favour aim-inhibited methods. There is, however, little in the youth culture of this country comparable to the North American dating institution as an acknowledged way of dealing with the problem of adolescent sexuality. Information

[1] Smith, op. cit., p. 77.

that is available is partial and clinical in nature. On the whole the topic is being faced more frankly than ever before but is one which still requires more factual information. If Kinsey's finding for America is true of this country, viz. that 'fifty per cent of the sex outlets of the male population are found in socially disapproved and largely illegal sources,'[1] then we can only assume that this involves extramarital intercourse on a much wider scale than many would like to believe, together with auto-erotic practices and homosexuality of varying kinds. Smith has argued that not only is sex the most discussed subject amongst teenage boys, but that 'there is an irreducible minimum of sexual secretion in young males that cannot be sublimated and will be released through direct sexual outlet.'[2]

It is surprising to find that resource to prostitutes is by no means confined in the United States to adult misfits or migrants and itinerants as we fondly imagine to be the case over here. That colonial immigrants, seafarers, alien servicemen, thwarted husbands and so on patronise our *maisons closes* we might be willing to allow. At the same time we would almost certainly protest against the suggestion that many university students or grammar school boys find their outlets through going with prostitutes. Yet Smith maintains that 'a summary of many studies reveals' in the U.S.A., at least, 'that fifty to seventy per cent of college males had premarital relations at some time, while a majority of the studies of college women record rates under thirty per cent.'[3] The deficit can be accounted for by the fact that middle class boys consort with lower class girls almost solely for the purpose of sexual experience (preferably with coitus, which confers considerable status) and that 'from fifty to eighty per cent of these boys reported visiting prostitutes.'

One suspects, but, of course, cannot prove, that in Britain auto-erotic practices and full or semi-homosexual activities are widespread and particularly prevalent in the higher income groups and in those who are confined to quasi-monastic educational establishments during this phase of their development. Moreover, we must not rule out an unknown minimal group who perhaps manage to control their urges until an appropriate time and age by the exercise of sheer will or self-control.

Furthermore, it is likely that some degree of sublimation, the release that is to say, of sex energies via substitute channelling

1 Smith, op. cit., p. 133.   2 Ibid., p. 131.   3 Ibid., p. 136.

activities is at least a possibility and that to some extent most young people, as most adults in fact, do achieve this. Self-display through dramatics, public debates, athletics and more creative outlets in painting, music, literature are all possible substitutes for direct sexual expression. Each may contribute to self-realisation, and, if not actually reduce the quantum of desire, can deflect interest and attention on to other things and by so doing lessen tension. Even for the better educated and more artistically inclined youths the possibility of finding adequate sublimations is, however, highly questionable.

As Dr Fleming has pointed out, the children from the poorest and most overcrowded homes suffer particularly from 'premature exposure' through lack of privacy.[1] As a result for this group 'there may be lost an expectation of anything other than the physical aspects of sexual relationships' which can lead to a rash choice of mate and a serious underestimation of the non-physical and purely companionate aspects of personal relationships between the partners.

Working class youths, hence, tend to rush into matrimony as a main means of gratifying sexuality at the physical level. The girls' problems are very different from the boys' but are, nevertheless, closely connected. 'In the main the chief problem for boys up to 17 years appeared to be masturbation. Those over 18 were mainly concerned with how far they should go in love-making, with questions about birth control, and how they could tell when and where a girl wanted them to stop. For girls the chief concern was how far to let a boy go?' So Jordan and Fisher summed up the situation in their perceptive study carried out with the members of their youth club after many long and frank discussions.[2]

The choice, then, largely dictated by social class position, seems in the main to lie between so-called perversions and precocity. At both ends of this spectrum there are dangers of gross promiscuity developing. Sexual desire, either 'normally' or abnormally attained and incontinently indulged in is likely to have unsettling consequences for future married relationships. Moreover, whatever adjustments young people make to their situation, all nowadays is

[1] Fleming, op. cit., p. 216.
[2] G. W. Jordan and E. M. Fisher, *Self-Portrait of Youth or the Urban Adolescent*; Heinemann, 1955, p. 119. The whole of the sixth chapter of this book, from which this quotation comes, entitled 'Sex and Maturity', deserves careful attention from all who have to deal professionally with young people and their needs.

enacted in an atmosphere of public titillation which encourages excess attention to the topic and leads directly into social pornography.[1]

Not only is much advertising steeped in manifest and hidden sexual appeals and incitements—so that even razor blades and boot polish are peddled by means of erotic imagery and carnal stimulation—but the visual arts, novels and magazines, by their continual attention to the same themes, tend to create an attitude of mind that regards all forms of sensuality as permitted, desirable and universally condoned. 'Only a fool would abstain' is one deduction youngsters might logically make. Or, if they are slightly more sophisticated, 'repression is wrong, free expression good for one's health.'

9

The question is often posed, why has organised dating on the transatlantic model not developed so much in Britain and is it not something which is likely to become prominent in the future? Is it not, moreover, an institution so clearly meeting a fundamental adolescent need that we ought to encourage its growth and foster it by every means in our power? Would it not be a much more honest approach to the problems of adolescent sexuality than the present confusion which can lead young people into serious difficulties through lack of socially accepted outlets.

My own view is that we may have to accept something of this nature as second best to control which would be too idealistic a solution. I merely wish at this point to suggest reasons why, as yet, the practice has been slow to catch on in Britain and to indicate those structural factors which are calculated to hinder its adoption. The major obstacle, as I see it, to institutionalised dating in British society is our ancient monosexual education and social traditions which not only colour people's ideas but have become

[1] The following coupled film titles running at city cinemas are good examples of the widespread physical excitation which is being commercially exploited in contemporary society:

Men Without Morals
Nudes in the Snow

Nudes of the World
The House of Sin

Nudist Paradise
The Naked Venus

heavily built into our institutional arrangements. Many English boys and girls spend much of their time in single sex schools and youth groups and the practice of co-education is still being met by a stubborn and powerful rearguard action from those traditionalists who still maintain the effective control of policy. American schools and colleges are commonly co-educational and as a consequence there has of necessity grown up in them a youth culture as opposed to a separate boy and a separate girl culture such as we know in this country. American boys and girls have been forced because of the prevailing educational policy to mix with each other and to work out some mutual *modus vivendi*. Segregation in Britain has worked, on the other hand, on the assumption of 'out of sight, out of mind.' Boys have been forbidden by their teachers to talk to girls and girls have similarly been banned from having anything overtly to do with boys. Even in some teacher training colleges the continuing *status pupilari* has permitted the administrators and the heads to exercise this benevolent protection over their students in the way of forbidding girls to have telephone conversations with men and other reactionary authoritarian devices. In educational circles in Britain sex is still regarded as something undesirable, and better not mentioned. *Solvitur ambulando;* or so some headmasters, headmistresses, college principals, directors of education and university dons have irresponsibly imagined. 'Cut them off from one another and let them burn. It will be good for their studies,' is the diehard theory which still, I think, represents a common view in this country even today. In fairness, one must admit that there are some signs of change. Some of the new training colleges are going to be co-educational. In many of the provincial universities men and women students share a common union. There are even the first brave beginnings of dual sex halls of residence. But grammar schools on the whole remain stoutly monosexual. Boarding schools (those founded on the orthodox public school model in particular) cling tenaciously to segregation with all the results in the way of dormitory malpractices and smaller boy 'tarts' which they officially deny but which nearly all ex-pupils blithely corroborate.

This is not the place to examine in detail the pros and cons of boarding school education either for the sons and daughters of middle class families or for the inmates of our penal establishments and other less fortunate youth. But it is clear that life in a segregated community must exert some influence on the growth of sexual ideas and relationships. These need not necessarily be regarded as deleterious but we must recognise the fact that in some British boarding schools even talking to members of the opposite sex is still regarded as a breach of discipline, which in boys' schools is frequently dealt with by the humiliating practice of corporal punishment. Such an attitude on the part of the adults in charge—to put the case as mildly as possible—cannot be said to constitute positive encouragement for the formation of a realistic and sensitive heterosexuality in the minds of the scholars. We would do well to recall in this connection the considered judgment of Dr Fleming to the effect that 'only within the flexibility of a genuine co-educational grouping can provision be made for informal opportunities for social learning for each boy or girl at the time which is most propitious.'[1]

The situation in Britain is hence at the moment fairly resistant to change but there are some signs that a youth culture on the American pattern may develop in the future. Youth organisations witness the clash of values acutely. While boys' clubs and scouts remain traditionally monosexual, girls' clubs are almost extinct and have sensibly given way before the pressure of youthful demand and generally turned themselves into 'mixed' clubs. Stalwarts of the boys' club and scouting movements may wish to preserve their boys from feminine advances as long as possible but in so doing they deceive themselves. The fact that nowadays boys over sixteen years of age are at best intermittent attenders at unisexual activities and at worst completely absent is widely admitted within the movements but not in public. Evidence made available to the Crowther Committee, however, when some thousand conscripts were interviewed, established beyond dispute that, of those young men who were still members of youth organisations at the age of eighteen, the majority were members of mixed groups.[2]

10

Coming to terms with the self demands then of the individual that he shall grow away, to some extent, from his family of origin, become less dependent on parents for guidance and affection and more autonomous on the one hand and more sensitive to the dictates and tastes of the peer group on the other. The individual must try to maintain friends of his own sex but also begin to make contact

[1] Fleming, op. cit., p. 157.   [2] *15 to 18*, op. cit., vol. i, p. 170.

socially and personally with members of the opposite sex. The move is outwards from the family and via the peer group or crowd towards the more enduring intimacies of heterosexual relationships. During the transition the influence of one's contemporaries is, if not paramount, then certainly immensely important. As David Riesman put it, at this stage 'if the adults are the judge, these peers are the jury.'[1] Adolescence is probably the stage, *par excellence*, of what he has encouraged us to call the other-directed personality. In the other-directed home the parents realise the significance of this and encourage their adolescents to mix and mingle with their contemporaries, lending them the physical means in the way of cash, motor-cars, the contents of the refrigerator and the exclusive use of the sitting-room for this purpose.

On the other hand, those homes which are inward-looking and jealously possessive in their emotional tone will, consciously or otherwise, set up a barrier to the growth of satisfying friendships for children either with members of their own or with the opposite sex.

The final stage of the adolescent phase might well be regarded as a point at which the individual has attained a psychological freedom and mental poise which makes marriage a possible and desirable future objective. The self image incorporates by this age the related concepts of matrimony and of paternity. By now young people may be said to have had the time to live through their developmental stage and to be nearing whatever we mean by maturity. Some of the questions life poses will by now have been answered. Some of the basic social and psychological tasks will have been attempted and mastered. A relative stability and self-assurance may have resulted from the successful issue of the problems and tasks set by the preceding decade. That striving for 'personal perfection' which Hemming[2] found to characterise the adolescents whose letters he analysed will have become adjusted to the realities of self and society, have passed out of the state of starry-eyed illusion and become anchored on the rock of firm moral principles and legitimate private ambitions.

It is quite clear that not everyone reaches this adult stability at the same chronological age. It is also equally apparent that some people

---

[1] David Riesman, *The Lonely Crowd*, abridged version; Doubleday Anchor Book, undated, p. 91.

[2] Hemming, op. cit., p. 171.

never achieve this ideal of maturity. The impact of irresponsible mass advertisement and commercial exploitation, the shortcomings of home and family life, the failures of school, church or youth organisation to nourish and guide the developing mind and character is shown in the illegitimacy rates, the broken marriages and the countless unsuitable partnerships of which every social worker and magistrate is acutely aware. The fact that advice and correspondence columns in the girls' comics and weeklies are flooded out with pathetic and sincere appeals for help and guidance, as Hemming said, far from giving us a picture of 'fecklessness, revolt, and disregard for accepted standards' reveals 'an ardent wish to master weaknesses' and suggests adult as well as juvenile and adolescent failure.[1]

At the risk of over-simplification and distortion we could perhaps best summarise what we have been saying in this chapter and its predecessor by suggesting for discussion the two different self images of boys and girls in our society which the available evidence has suggested.

Girls see their social role to be intimately bound up with marriage and home making. Even middle class girls who have received college and high school or grammar school and university training seem to regard the roles of mother and wife as of no less and probably of more importance than that of professional worker.[2]

However, the evidence which was incorporated in the now famous Crowther Report is not entirely substantiated by a most interesting enquiry which was recently undertaken amongst the ex-pupils of Bolton School.[3] This Report showed that of the '56 girls who had left between 1954 and 1959 only ten are married already' (i.e. by 1960), 'and none of these less than three years after leaving. . . . This tendency in our respondents to postpone marriage is no doubt connected with the remarkable fact that of all those who took further training—i.e. 237 out of a total of 250—only two failed to complete their course.'

This would seem to suggest that for the girls who are products of schools with high academic standards, well in advance of the average grammar school even, matrimony is thought of as a second stage to be undertaken *after* a professional qualification has been

1 Hemming, op. cit., p. 171.   2 Cf. Seeley, *et al.*, op. cit., pp. 181–2.
3 *Learning and Living, A Feminine Viewpoint*, Bolton School Old Girls' Association, privately printed, undated.

gained. Thereafter they seem to fall into the general trend, marrying in fact 'within three or four years of graduation.'

Such a well disciplined life-plan, however, is not likely to be the common lot of the vast majority of girls in our community for a very long time to come. It represents a rational and economically very sound attitude to life on the part of the young women concerned, and one can only hope that there will be many more schools like Bolton to build up a similar tradition in the future. It is a response to the truth embodied in the comment of a husband, quoted in the report which distils the essence of sensible middle class culture: 'No family can really develop fully unless both parents are of equal intellectual attainment.'

For the girls who do not succeed academically or who do positively badly at school early marriage is the main avenue of social and economic advancement.[1] The wifely and maternal roles are the traditional feminine ones in our society and women on the whole achieve status mainly via their husbands. A slow revolution is, of course, in progress which is drastically undermining this long established relative position of the sexes. It is already discernible in middle class and middle income groups but is making, for obvious reasons, rather heavier weather in working class cultures. Women's achievement of equal status with men, although far from realised, is opening up exciting new social vistas for both sexes. The fact that economically women are now well able to maintain themselves, even, in some professions, to achieve supremacy over male colleagues, coupled with the power to limit pregnancy at will, is tending to make men and women not only more equal but their roles more similar. A greater measure of interchangeability of role is likely to result from this revolution, together with increasing flexibility and sympathy in interpersonal relationships.

Equality, however, does not mean identity. Male and female roles and their related ideologies will diverge at specific points, especially during the years of elected child-bearing and while the children are at the nursery stage of development. Thereafter there is likely to be a closer *rapprochement* but it is still obvious that in many walks of life and in some professional careers women never succeed in re-establishing themselves entirely *vis-à-vis*

---

[1] See Havighurst, *et al.*, op. cit., pp. 128–9.

their male coevals. There are still sturdy remnants of a formerly totally male-dominated culture existing today. Nevertheless, the trend is obvious enough and its significance for the future cannot be denied.

Boys, on the other hand, are never in doubt as to their ultimate objective. Even in the infants' school they are made to realise that men go out to work, to earn the family bread and butter, and that this is a lifelong process, interrupted only by illness or the sack. Boys are hence career-oriented from the start and seldom if ever are they allowed to take their eyes off the target. During schooldays the drill of examinations prepares them for the world of competitive collaboration which they will have to enter and spend the rest of their lives in. A boy looks forward to being both worker and husband, and, more remotely, father. He is used to the idea of the family centred on its home-ground as a 'consumption unit' for which he will have to supply the main source of the financial means. He is conditioned to the idea that his wife will look after him to some extent physically, bear his children and afford companionship and support. An agreed division of labour exists between them, justified now more on grounds of expediency than of immutable law, so that he will be prepared at times to look after or help in the care of the children and even to participate in household chores such as shopping, cooking and cleaning. Again middle class youths have moved much further than their working class counterparts in the direction of accepting an easy and flexible division of labour in the family, but even among the latter there are indications that the rising generations have moved some way from the more inflexible differential role system of their parents' and grandparents' days.

In the adolescent phase, it is possible to distinguish the preparation for adult life taking place differentially between boys and girls. But the preparation is, as already indicated, one for what may be called 'differential equality,' not for full identity which would make nonsense of biological distinctions nor for the dominance-submission relationship of former times. So far in this country this change is no more than a trend, especially observable in middle class families. Even in the United States, which has moved further in most directions than we have, it was still possible—until recently anyway — to detect significant differences between occupational classes with regard to an individual's relations with school, church, job, recreation, the peer group and his own family of origin and of pro-creation.[1]

Coleman's findings for the pupils attending the ten schools in the Chicago area that he studied pinpoint differences between boys' and girls' attitudes during the adolescent phase which are obviously related to their somewhat dissimilar concepts of their future destinies.[2]

Possessing a good personality was the most important factor associated with being in the leading set amongst the girls. Good looks came second, and having nice clothes and being smart and well-dressed third. Coleman identified the leading crowd primarily in terms of being good looking and dateable, or, wherever ascriptive values were held to be important and connected to family background, in cruder terms of money and kinship standing. Boys, on the other hand, favoured athletic success as the key to being members of the leading crowd. Academic success, although not so important as athletic achievement, was more useful for boys than for girls. But the mere possession of certain equipment, e.g. free use of the family car, was also a valued factor making for social success and acceptability with the peer group. Boys on the whole were found to value a person for his achievements in work or sport, putting physical attributes lower on their list, whereas girls tended to rate good looks, personality, charm and so forth more highly. For girls there was nothing to compare with athletics for the boys, unless perhaps being a 'cheer leader' at college. Coleman suggests that the emphasis amongst girls on such 'superficial, external attributes' as 'clothes and good looks' pervades the adolescent culture to such an extent that this tends, in the end, to be 'the only basis or the *most important* basis on which to excel',[3] with not entirely satisfactory results. This might, indeed, be one outcome of co-education. Thus by putting boys and girls closely together during the time when they are most likely to be interested in one another as potential partners may not always promote, as it is so often claimed, 'adjustment to life; it may promote, as indicated by these data, adjustment to the life of a model or chorus girl or movie actress or call girl. It may, in other words, promote *mal*adjustment to the kind of life that these girls will lead after school.'[4]

[1] See Hollingshead, op. cit., especially pp. 439–53. Coleman's enquiry, some decade or so later, does not confirm Hollingshead's in a number of important ways, however.   [2] Coleman, op. cit.   [3] Ibid., p. 52.   [4] Ibid., p. 52.

A further undesirable result of excessive attention to good looks and an attractive physical appearance is the dissatisfaction, sometimes experienced to the point of sheer anguish, felt by those youngsters who know they lack the requisite charm and beauty to evoke instant attention and interest. Those who suffer from some actual abnormality or maculation, sometimes even imperfect eyesight, can often be cast into the depths of despair over their shortcomings. The result is often an obsessional attention to cosmetics coupled with severe inferiority feelings which not only make for tense and irritable social relations but seriously impair the ego-ideal. It is necessary for young people to come to terms with themselves at all levels if they are to achieve the poise and stability of personality which are essential if any kind of happiness is to be their lot. They have to accept themselves 'warts and all' if they are ever to mature fully. Limitations of a physical nature are often harder to accept and tolerate than those of an intellectual character. This in itself is a commentary on both the adolescent culture and the values of the wider society in which it is embedded, that superficial appearances are so often given a higher rating than intangible moral and spiritual qualities of character. Unless a man loves himself (i.e. has an honest concern for his own nature, attributes and needs) he will never learn to love another being to the full.

Flann and Mary Campbell in an article contributed to *New Society* have analysed a number of girls' magazines in an attempt to assess the images presented for emulation, and concluded that 'the moral code' presented by them 'is a curious mixture of titillation and suburban gentility. Sex is all-pervading, but never goes beyond kissing and cuddling. The heroine is sweetly pretty, docile and a bit of a prude.'[1] The social background of the characters presented in these publications is 'almost always upper working class or lower middle class, that is socially slightly superior to the reader's own class, and the glamour jobs are as models, air hostesses or secretaries in TV and film studios.'[2] My colleague in the university, Mrs Carol Owen, in a study of feminine roles assessed quantitatively by content analysis of a number of women's periodicals similarly concluded that 'the image of the acceptable woman as

[1] Flann and Mary Campbell, 'Comic Love', *New Society* (No. 14), 3, January, 1963, pp. 24–25.
[2] Ibid.

projected by the fiction of women's weekly magazines is that of a parasite.'[1]

While, as Mrs Owen cogently points out, this image is to a considerable extent compensatory and serves as some kind of fantasy fulfilment for women who have not achieved a high degree of emotional satisfaction in their own private lives, there can be little doubt that working class feminine models are nearer to the concept of the domestic courtesan than of the female colleague or equal marriage partner. Glamour and man-appeal are too much emphasised at the expense of sterner qualities of character and young women are perhaps encouraged to concentrate more on attraction than on affinity. Middle class girls show up rather better. They are rather more likely to emphasise the importance of academic achievement, of entrance to a career and of selecting the right partner in marriage.[2]

The movement in the direction of married adulthood is hence both aided and impeded by attention to sexual appeal. Many years ago, however, Dr Macalister Brew drew our attention to the fact that young people evidence a healthy and rational interest in the whole business of personal relationships.[3] A recent investigation carried out by E. M. Eppel of London University draws attention to the same reassuring fact. Eppel concluded on the basis of the evidence derived from a study of knowledgeable adults' answers to his questions that 'the quality of personal relations seem to be the main touchstone for their assessment of their own and others' moral standards.'[4]

As long as personal relationships are regarded and treated as primary and fundamental there is hope of greater equality between the sexes and a higher degree of married compatibility being attained. There is more likelihood of young people coming to evaluate one another on grounds of behaviour rather than of class or social status, of them taking one another on their individual merits apart from ascriptive qualities. Marriage and stable friendship can only exist in our kind of society on the basis of personal affection and moral esteem. What people are like, in the final analysis, ought to matter more than who they are.

[1] Carol Owen, 'Feminine Roles and Social Mobility in Women's Weekly Magazines', *The Sociological Review*, vol. 10, No. 3, Nov. 1962, pp. 283–96.

[2] Cf. Veness, op. cit., pp. 129–34.

[3] J. Macalister Brew, *In the Service of Youth*; Faber and Faber, 1943.

[4] E. M. Eppel, 'Adolescent Values', *New Society*, (No. 26), 28th March, 1963, p. 10.

Adolescent concern with personal relationships stems from a growing and deepening sense at that time of personal identity. The two realisations—that of self and other selves—grow side by side and mutually support each other. This is one of the reasons why adolescence has traditonally been regarded as a time of flowering, of emotional and creative sensitivity and their correlative needs for expressive outlets. Art, literature, religion, moral fervour, the pursuit of the ideal and championship of noble causes are all traditionally associated with this stage at which the need to love and to be loved becomes increasingly important. It is hence the hour of supreme optimism and idealism and thus of the darkest potentiality for abysmal despair.

1

If adolescence is a terminal developmental stage, then post-adolescence signals the beginning of adulthood. It is the last major step towards ultimate maturity. It is the time when the self-image is realised in some of its fullness, when the readiness for genital experience has to be harmonised with the psyche's expanding spirituality. The concept of maturity thus envisaged is both psychological and physical. Physiological and psychological elements intermingle and reinvigorate one another. Neither must be stressed to the point at which the other is relatively excluded. Moreover, the whole process must always be seen as taking place within a social context. Thus a mature individual is one who succeeds in resolving the problems presented to him by the particular culture in which he happens to live. Growing up and attaining a level of development which can be termed mature, therefore, entails a harmonious socio-psycho-biological process over a number of years. There are difficulties to be resolved at all points. Growth cannot be expected to follow a uniform and uninterrupted rhythm. There will be ups and downs, advances and partial retreats along the way. Tremendous variations will occur between individuals, and individuals themselves will not always be advancing at the same pace. Generalisation in these circumstances is risky and appeals to the average and comparisons against the so-called normal pattern of growth and development can gravely mislead teachers and parents.

Indeed, the very concept of maturity may be something of a chimera. The idea that we reach a point of stability at a specific moment of time, when all our inherent qualities achieve full expression and all social demands are serenely and competently met, can be a dangerous illusion. The so-called normal man may prove to be as deadly and dreary a personality as the colourless residuum of prolonged psychoanalytical treatment—all passion spent, and so delicately walking the tightrope between expression and repression that the personality declines into a dull unadventurous respectability, which is in itself a mockery of all we mean by living a full life. 'In one sense,' an anonymous psychiatrist admitted in a broadcast talk, 'we need our immaturities. Although we may present an adult mask to the world, in most of us there is a child who never quite grows up. We may deplore our childishness; but we need it to keep us alive.'[1]

Thus the idea of the perfectly poised, integrated, balanced personality which has put aside childish things, suffers from no illusions, is tolerant of frustration and conflicting views, is not driven by excess ambitions or given over to irrational anxieties, may be thought of as a general direction rather than as a precise road to be followed, a compass point not an entire map of life. It is yonder shining light to which we are called, not a detailed set of rules of the road.

It is equally apparent that the area that we are now entering presents unusual difficulties today for the young and for older folk as well. To put it in somewhat outmoded terms what we mean here by 'coming to terms with life as a whole,' involves what people rather pompously used to call 'finding a philosophy of life,' or, more narrowly, a religion or, at least, a set of values to live by. One thing is quite certain; we cannot avoid the issue. As Carlyle said to the lady who informed him that on the whole she found that she was prepared to accept the universe, 'By God, madam, you had better!'

We have indeed no choice but to take life on its own terms, but each individual, one supposes, struggles with the experience and tries to wrestle some sense or idea of purpose and meaning from the long and bitter battle.

To a considerable extent the growth of sexuality at adolescence promotes religious and philosophical development. The sex drive which entails both maternal and paternal feelings in addition to the desire to love and be loved by an equal partner forces the individual to think less of himself and more of the needs of others. Indeed it is the growth of love which alone makes the growth of religion possible. Our religious ideas are saturated in emotions which derive much of their strength from sexuality and the desire to produce and nurture offspring. The roots of religion are grounded in the altruism which the onset of sexuality has begun to create.

It is indeed doubtful whether a young child can ever love in the full sense of that term. Love, as Simey has recently argued in relation to the care and education of deprived children, is closer to the Christ-

[1] 'What is Psychological Maturity?', *The Listener*, June 14, 1962, pp. 1030-31.

ian *agape* than to the Freudian *eros*.[1] He quotes Dr Harry Stack Sullivan in corroboration:

The capacity to love in its initial form makes appearance as the mark of one who has ceased to be juvenile and has become pre-adolescent. . . . When the satisfaction or the security of another person becomes as significant to one as is one's own satisfaction or security, then the state of love exists.[2]

Sullivan's concept is, of course, an ideal one and it may be doubted whether any of us (saints apart) ever truly comes to love another human being in that fullness, although this is the goal to which, in our best moments, we may consciously strive to attain. But it also seems clear from Suttie's work that love has its roots way back in early childhood and does not spring fully mature from the psyche at adolescence.[3] The capacity to respond to affection and to reciprocate it, even to cherish a love object without any Freudian ambivalence, is by no means unusual in childhood and even in infancy.

But after puberty it seems that the individual adds to his growing capacity for reciprocity of affection, developing sentiments of protective and parental concern, as, impelled on the deep rhythms of sexuality, he moves towards mating and procreation. The final experience of parenthood opens up an understanding of what the saints mean when they speak of the Fatherhood of God. To become a parent is almost a mystical experience even for agnostics and unbelievers.[4]

2

Some writers would want to distinguish between religion and philosophy of life, implying perhaps that the former necessarily involves relationship with deity. I would not myself wish to make such a distinction. I tend to the view that, for the great majority of mankind, the business of acquiring a set of values is inextricably bound up with more or less formal religious teaching in childhood and that most of us, in fact, never unravel the two. As far as British

[1] T. S. Simey, *The Concept of Love in Child Care*, National Children's Home Memorial Lecture, Convocation, 1960.

[2] Ibid., p. 56.

[3] Ian Suttie, *The Origins of Love and Hate*; Kegan Paul, 1935; Penguin Books, 1960.

[4] Cf. Oswald Schwarz, *The Psychology of Sex*; Penguin Books, 1949, p. 62, '. . . sexuality leads the adolescent to God—and not the other way round.'

142 THE YOUNG PRETENDERS

society is concerned it seems inevitable that religious ideas, moral
values and ethical principles are first implanted and stirred in us in
a religious or quasi-religious context. That is to say ideas of right
and wrong, good and evil are first presented within a metaphysical
framework and in relation to the will and action of God defined
more or less in terms of the Bible and Christian tradition.

Dr Wall in a brief but invaluable discussion of this aspect of the
individual's maturation has spoken of adolescence as 'the period
of "turning the world upside down," of self-dedication to a cause
or an idea, political or social, of religious conversion, of the attempt
to generalise specific truths and to form from them a philosophy
of life.'[1] He suggests that 'altruistic idealism' should become the
master sentiment thereafter. The task of home, school and church
at this time is to assist this progress towards the achievement of 'a
coherent scheme of values.'

It is possible, and, for the mystically-inclined, fatally easy, to talk
and write a great deal of airy nonsense on this topic. School teachers
who themselves possess a firm religious faith are often among the
most deluded in this respect. They imagine that by making the
chapel central to the life of the school sturdy young Christians can be
spiritually nurtured and that there will be a direct transference of
the values presented in confirmation class to the conduct of everyday
life. Thomas Arnold, I suppose, was one of the great pioneers of
this view-point which, since his day, has permeated public school
education and through the pervasive influence of ex-public school
boy headmasters exerted an immense impact on the ethos of the
typical grammar school.

Adherents of particular Christian sects lay great emphasis on the
need to educate their children in their own denominational schools.
Roman Catholics are adamant on the subject. So, too, are many
Anglicans and Non-conformists. Presumably children who derive
from families which are actively associated with one denomination
or another see to it that their children receive both moral instruction,
theological teaching and initiation into the practices of their specific
faith. They give their children religious experience at home, at
church and at school. The vast majority, however, attend state schools
but even there in Britain religious knowledge has a legitimised place
in the curriculum and every morning there is prescribed 'collective
worship,' when hymns are sung, prayers recited, scriptural passages

[1] Wall, *Education and Mental Health*, op. cit., p. 149.

read aloud and possibly some kind of moral homily expounded by the Head. In the main, therefore, it can be claimed that all pupils at English schools are regularly exposed to ethical and religious influences, unless of course their parents opt out, and that children who attend denominational schools get rather more instruction than the majority. Broadly speaking, we can say that everybody is exposed to Christian influence and has an opportunity to understand something of the Christian view of life. To this extent, then, we can claim that this is a Christian country and that Christian values contribute powerfully to the general climate of ideas and to some extent condition the social norms of most groups.

These Christian values and concepts, however imperfectly conveyed and however imperfectly understood, help to mould our way of life and colour our conduct and social institutions. For the minority there is indoctrination in the faith of a particular sect or denomination; for the majority there is a kind of generalised, diffuse school-Christianity which is not related to the practice of any worshipping community.

When we ask what the outcome of all this is, we come up against almost overwhelming difficulties. Nobody in fact knows, although there are many and various opinions. Empirical research has hardly begun to grapple with the gigantic task of attempting to assess or even understand what is happening, although here and there some small scale spot studies have been made. But no social scientist has yet had the courage to follow in the footsteps of the redoubtable Charles Booth and undertake today a similar broadly based enquiry into the religious influences acting upon a sizeable body of people at a particular moment in their history.

Booth's *Religious Influences* enquiry carried out at the end of the nineteenth century in London was originally concerned to discover the extent people accepted doctrine and shared in the work of the various religious bodies in operation at that time. It involved long interviews with the leaders of every religious body other than the Jews, interminable perusal of magazines and reports and a tremendous number of actual visits to churches, chapels and meeting houses. The product of these painstaking enquiries filled many notebooks and by the end of the year 1900, Booth addressed himself to the arduous task of writing it all up in a form suitable for publication. Simey has described this as 'an especially difficult and tormenting experience,'[1] not least because Booth himself was emotionally involved (as almost any honest research worker would have been) with the subject of the enquiry. The picture of religious life which Booth finally presented to his fellow countrymen 'was a depressing one, though Booth did not so regard it himself.'[2] Depressing, that is to say, to those who might have believed all was well with the religious life of the nation but a picture which would most certainly have confirmed the ideas of the professional sociologist. Booth was led to conclude 'that the churches had adapted themselves to the class structure, rather than acted as a force transforming it. Each class had a church which catered for its needs, though most of the working class held aloof altogether.' While it was the Evangelical churches which held most sway over the vast bulk of lower class people, 'the average working man did not feel inclined to give up the simple pleasures and sins to which he was accustomed, and so far as guilt was concerned, his political leaders were busy convincing him that he was more sinned against than sinning.'[3]

Booth found, then, that the churches had in the main lost contact with the majority of people at that time and that their activities were largely irrelevant to the events that were taking place in society. Socialism was really taking over from the Church as the vital spiritual motivating force in contemporary society. Booth had no palliatives to offer the folk who deplored this state of affairs. The drift away from organised religion seems to have proceeded apace during the years that followed until today, it may fairly be claimed, church attendance and active membership are confined to no more than a quarter of the population. The middle classes seem to be following the working classes in a general withdrawal from the churches, although here and there in particular localities largish congregations may still be found and the allegiance of the Roman Catholics, though reduced, is by no means in eclipse.

I am aware that in this section I am entering upon highly controversial ground and that emotions will be stirred one way or the other by whatever is said. But as far as Britain is concerned, I should have thought that both church adherents and those who remain sympathetically aloof would be ready to agree to the following propositions:

---

[1] T. S. and M. B. Simey, *Charles Booth, Social Scientist*, Oxford, 1960, p. 145.
[2] Ibid., p. 149.   [3] Ibid., pp. 149–50.

1. There has been a very substantial falling off in church allegiance during the past fifty years.

2. Church attendance is no longer the hallmark of respectability nor is there any social prestige attached to church-going or to church membership; on the contrary, those who still remain in membership often find themselves regarded as old fogies and kill-joys.

3. There are no indications that there is likely to be any reversal of the trend in the next decade or so.

The situation in the United States would seem to be rather different. There something like half the population is said to attend religious worship, while there are many examples of full congregations and prosperous churches. It would be a gross mistake, however, to assume for this reason that the people of America are basically more religious than Britishers. Nor, moreover, would it be fair to deduce, merely from the statistics of church attendance, that Americans are more moral, either in their average behaviour or in their general attitudes, than are British people. Indeed much of the evidence from the U.S.A. would seem to suggest that church-going and religious affiliations are taken somewhat lightly and that the social side is more important than doctrinal or theological implications. William H. Whyte's study of the 'church of suburbia' suggests that membership of a church meets contemporary middle class people's needs for group experience and that, in so far as the churches can supply this basic need for fellowship, they are widely supported.[1] Doctrinal differences in the posh suburb of Park Forest are taken so lightly that it has been possible for most of the Protestant denominations to pass over their differences and club together to support one big, happy, united Protestant church partly on the logical grounds of 'Why give small salaries to five so-so pastors instead of a decent salary to one good one?'[2] This is probably not indicative of any profound movement in the direction of a reunited Christendom. At the same time it should not be dismissed as nothing more than social gregariousness and the retreat from loneliness. One thing, surely, any church ought to be is a community of people. If it is not that it is a long way short of fulfilling its spiritual, let alone its other, functions. Whyte comes to the guarded conclusion that 'the quest among the transients for a socially useful church is a deeply felt one. They do not seek fellowship simply because they

---

1 William H. Whyte, *The Organization Man*, Cape, 1957: Penguin Books, 1960.
2 Ibid., Penguin edition, p. 340.

cannot avoid the need. They seek it actively, and they feel that it is ultimately a moral quest.'[1]

This point, which may be somewhat baffling for the less socialised English, seems to me to be valid. The search for fellowship can indeed be deeply related to men's spiritual needs and to their quest for a set of moral values to live their lives by. It can equally represent nothing more than a hearty sociability or a frightened gregariousness. There is no objective way of knowing either individually or collectively. But if people find their fellowship within the church or chapel rather than in the club or pub it suggests that they are in pursuit, however dimly and fumblingly, of something more than mateyness, something greater than cosiness, although fellowship and cosiness are among the ends that many worshippers seek. But, in England at any rate, there is little or no social kudos to be derived from going to church or chapel. Those who do attend seek other than status ends, and it is surely conceivable that amongst these many ends there may be some which are related to 'the Christian way of life' and to the search for moral values and imperatives. It is also conceivable that the attempt to create and participate in a certain kind of fellowship, even though we dare not attach to this any grandiloquent title like the 'kingdom of right relationships,' is a religious as well as a social activity. Some sociologists, of course, would regard these as indistinguishable. They would say that religious activities are always and only social in nature and origin although none the less important for all that, exercising a merely cohesive and emotional or euphoric function. Some, indeed, would go further along the same road with Emile Durkheim and declare that men derive their very concept of the divine from the nature of society, and that in what they imagine to be their seeking for God they are in reality merely responding to the social element in human experience.[2] Other sociologists disagree with this assertion and would claim that religion by its very nature is not a proper object for empirical investigation, and that, while certain forms of religious behaviour are susceptible to sociological study, religion itself, in the last analysis, cannot be brought within the scope of scientific enquiry because it involves elements of mysticism which place it in a unique category.

[1] William H. Whyte, *The Organization Man*, Penguin edition, p. 351.
[2] Emile Durkheim, *The Elementary Forms of the Religious Life*, first published in English in 1915, is a *locus classicus* of many of these functionalist interpretations of the nature and significance of religious behaviour.

It is fortunately not necessary to take sides in this controversy here, but we can take it for granted that most so-called religious activities do contain social components and that what is sometimes referred to as 'contemporary man's thirst for community' is to a considerable extent a religious and a moral experience. Furthermore, the stress which young people tend to place upon personal relationships, to which past and present research workers have drawn our attention, is probably closely associated with this groping after true fellowship and the expression of what we may legitimately call a spiritual hunger. Those who wish may draw some solace, then, from the idea that, although there are indications that organised religion is weakening its hold on the population and formal worship is on the decrease in our society, other moral and spiritual elements which are truly religious in nature are far from being denigrated or denied. The one, in fact, may prove to be the complement of the other and reciprocally related to it: as the tide of formal religious affirmation ebbs, the waves of concern for persons and for the quality of personal relationships comes flooding in to replace what has gone or been lost.

We may conclude by saying that religious and essentially Christian values are alive in our social climate, that most youngsters are touched at some time of their lives, both formally and informally, by these values, and that they are usually taken into account by any individual in search of a philosophy of living. These Christian values, however, are far from being universal or predominant. Other values and notions contend with them for supremacy. A good deal of lip-service is paid to Christian standards which undoubtedly is harmful both for the Christian religion and for social morality. One would also hazard the guess that there are not many people nowadays who take religious values or moral principles very seriously in deciding on their personal actions. The religious values and the moral principles are still spoken of, they are still part of the air we breathe, but, in the final issue, it is almost impossible to think of, say, a British cabinet coming to a policy decision on these grounds alone. Most of us are influenced, consciously and unconsciously, directly and indirectly, by the ethical values associated with the Christian church's teaching and by the values and attitudes portrayed in the Gospel accounts of the life of Jesus, but they do not play an overriding part in decision-making or action as far as the great majority of us go. Social and economic considerations, common sense and expediency dictate most of what we do. Young people learn this at a fairly early age and reproduce the kind of behaviour their elders and social superiors have taught them.

3

Several community studies, mostly carried out in North America, have dealt with the way values are acquired and what part definitely 'religious' behaviour seems to play in the life of the individual and the social group. Hollingshead devoted a chapter to 'Religion and Religious Behavior' in his study of Elmtown. His findings are hardly encouraging for the devout. 'The impression gradually grew,' he tells us, 'that religion to these adolescents is comparable in a way to wearing clothes or taking a bath. It is something one had to do to become acceptable in society.'[1] Thus for the bulk of youth, 90 per cent of the boys and 80 per cent of the girls studied, religion had no compulsive quality and they thought, if in religious traditional terms at all, very nebulously. The one thing in Elmtown not to do was to say one was either an atheist or a Communist. To do so would brand an individual as an outsider and possibly even as an enemy of society. A mild degree of conformity is enjoined, with the result that most of the youngsters think of the local church as 'a community facility like the school, the drug store, the city government, the bowling alley,' without, one presumes, any supernatural quality. Young people attend without being moved. They are far from experiencing moral doubts or religious crises. 'It is plain,' Hollingshead concluded, 'that about 7 out of 8 young people are not troubled by religious questions or problems.'[2] The minority who did experience such problems were mainly Norwegian Lutherans.

Hollingshead reports a fair degree of tension between the school teachers and the local pastors arising out of contradictions between the differential instruction given in these two institutions to which the children are culturally exposed. Ministers exhort their flock to rely upon providence and prayer to resolve their difficulties, while the guidance given in the classrooms often has a much more rationalistic basis. Hollingshead cites the case of a devout Lutheran boy who believed, on the strength of what he had learned either at church or in Sunday School, that a flood which inundated the district in the year 1942 was a divine punishment for America's entry into the war

[1] Hollingshead, op. cit., p. 244.   [2] Ibid., p. 246.

against Germany and Japan. A Free Methodist girl thought prayer could have averted this local disaster. She was told by her teacher that there were no such things as miracles and a parochial crisis ensued. The minister accused the local High School of teaching 'blasphemous rot.' Obviously at that time the relationship between the church leaders and the more rationalistic and scientific minded school teachers was far from being an easy one, and, from time to time, pressure was brought by conservative critics on the school board superintendent to discipline recalcitrant pedagogues.

Reference has already been made to a similar cultural disharmony in Seeley's *Crestwood Heights* study. The authors pointed out that the logic of the religious truths inculcated in church demand a social order other than that in existence.[1] A society based on competition (however politely veiled) and on class stratification can hardly be regarded as a sound foundatoin for the erection of the Kingdom of Heaven on earth. Seeley points out that children are exposed to two sometimes conflicting ideologies, both of which must be accepted as valid but only one of which in effect is to be put into practice in the organisation of private life and public affairs. Equality and brotherhood are to be espoused as spiritual ideals and bowed down to in church but are not to be allowed to infiltrate into the social structure. Society must in fact be preserved from the implementation of the religious ideals it gives deference to in a specifically religious context. The two spheres—social and religious—must be kept more or less rigidly separate in hermetically sealed compartments.

The attempt to keep religious values away from every-day, and especially economic, affairs is not always a complete success. One of the ways of keeping the peace between the conflicting claims of the two ideologies is by coming to rely more and more on experts in all walks of life. The expert, cast for a messianic role, helps the troubled conscience to cope with the more obvious inconsistencies between belief and action. Thus we can appreciate the important role played by the expert today, especially in the field of Mental Health as keeper of the public and private conscience.

To return to Elmtown, however, we find that Hollingshead largely confirmed Charles Booth's findings for London at the turn of the century. 'From the stand-point of class position,' he declared, 'the lower the level the higher is the incidence of non-affiliation'

---

[1] Seeley, *et al.*, op. cit., p. 401 *et seq.*

with any worshipping body.[1] Or to put it another way round: 'the higher the class level the larger is the proportion of attendance' at Sunday worship as far as the adolescents were concerned.[2] The same conclusion is reached after examining the membership of youth groups sponsored by a church: 'the lower a boy's or girl's class position is, the higher the probability that he or she does not belong to a religious club.'[3]

Most of the ministers of Elmtown churches like those interviewed by Miss Jean Hill in her Liverpool enquiry were troubled by adolescent defection from their congregations and inclined to complain bitterly about it.[4] Their critical attitude is seen to be based on a gross misreading of the actual situation and to arise largely from holding strong *a priori* views on how children ought to behave and what their proper relation should be with the ordained ministry. Dr Joan Brothers in her study of secondary grammar school leavers and university students in Liverpool encountered a similarly set attitude on the part of the priests she interviewed. She found that they complained bitterly about grammar school and university students disassociating themselves from parochial activities, although the evidence did not support the wholesale withdrawal that their strictures suggested.[5]

Clergy, in the main, expect that people will go to church; indeed they go much further and demand it as a sacred duty, and anyone who does not attend or who attends services only but opts out of all other parochial duties is letting them and the church down. Television, too much pocket money, the Welfare State itself, comparative affluence and economic security are all singled out for attack by the clergy as conducing to young people's lukewarm attitude towards church association. Hollingshead raps them smartly over the knuckles for this ignorant and unsympathetic approach to youth.

In their relations with adolescents, these ministers fail to realise the following three facts about the churches they lead and the cultural system in which they function: first, no church has adapted its service to the needs of this age group; second, the adolescents have transformed the young

[1] Hollingshead, op. cit., p. 249.   [2] Ibid., p. 251.   [3] Ibid., p. 253.
[4] The reference is to an unpublished enquiry based mainly on interviews with 140 school leavers in Liverpool. Miss Hill interviewed local priests and parsons and found that very many of them looked upon adolescence as a time of religious disruption.
[5] Joan Brothers, *Church and School*; Liverpool University Press, 1964.

people's groups into semi-private clubs, and the students who run them extend the class system into the churches on the adolescent level; third, the ministers by their attitude towards the behaviour of the adolescents build a barrier between themselves and their adolescent members.[1]

Once again we touch on the way in which the realities of the social world work against the parsons in their attempt to create a truly Christian institution within the existing framework of a highly secular society. Hollingshead suggests that many priests and pastors simply refuse to face the facts of real life and bury their heads in the sands in an effort to prevent this tension coming to full consciousness. The Methodist minister, worried by youngsters' withdrawal, nevertheless stubbornly denied that the reason could in any way be attributed to 'the influence of class on religious behaviour when the question was raised.' The Lutheran ministers, advancing an extreme puritanical view-point, forced the youthful members of their congregations into a kind of double standard of behaviour. Forbidden by precept and injunction to enjoy the pleasures of world and flesh, many nevertheless participated in the tabooed activities but kept quiet about it. The Roman Catholic priest took a much more sensible and realistic view of human nature. 'As far as he was concerned, the role of the church was not to suppress human desires, but to provide young persons with a solid anchorage upon which they could base their hopes for salvation in the hereafter.'[2]

Catholics, then, were not confronted with the need to dissemble or to practice a double morality and we may presume that for this reason they had less troubled consciences than the Lutherans and were the better for it.

The general picture presented by the Elmtown study is one of limited acceptance and conformity, on the one hand, and of downright spiritual dishonesty on the other. Most of the students professed to believe in God and considered themselves Christians in a vague and generalised way.[3] Something like half of them took part in religious activities but participation was definitely class-biased and many more middle class than lower class youngsters were associated with a worshipping community. Moreover, a psychological

[1] Hollingshead, op. cit., p. 257.   [2] Ibid., p. 265.
[3] A recent study of English grammar school pupils showed that something like 75 per cent seemed to believe in the existence of God but of this number no more than half were in the habit of attending church or performing private devotions. See D. S. Wright, 'Research and Studies', University of Leeds, Institute of Education, vol. 24.

barrier seemed to divide the youth from the ministry of which the latter seemed oblivious. The young people mainly went their own way, banding together in clusters to 'do what their class and age groups do,' and, if caught doing things tabooed by the ministers, they either withdrew altogether from church activities or, more generally, hid this side of their lives 'from the minister, as they do from their teachers and parents, and happily' went 'with the crowd.'[1]

Havighurst and his collaborators found in River City that there was also 'a marked relation between church participation and social class, with higher-status youth much more active in church.'[2] They found further that there was a relationship between school progress, higher intelligence and being interested in formal religion, 'with those who get the most education being the more interested.' The authors of the River City survey expressed uncertainty in interpreting their findings. One view, they point out, could be that 'the church is doing a good job for those with whom it comes into contact,' while on the other hand they pointed out that 'another person may say that these findings indicate that the church mainly serves those who need it least, those who are higher in social status and who are already getting along well in school and community'.[3]

They do not find much evidence, however, to support that idea of 'the redeeming power of the church in River City.' Nevertheless, it is clear that a number of boys and girls are helped by being associated with one or other denomination, and the fact that 'two-thirds of the church youth leaders are not school leaders indicates that the church supplies something important for this group.'[4] The final impression, then, is one of limited success and influence. Probably the ones who receive most from their church membership and attendance do so because of their family background, but the claim that is often made that organised religion exerts a transforming influence on the community as a whole is not substantiated while there are so many socially unsuccessful or indifferently successful youngsters outside its ministrations altogether.

Turning to current British investigations we note that Leslie Wilkins in his 1950 enquiry, in answer to the precise question 'Would you mind telling me how you actually spent last Sunday morning?,' which at best can only be regarded as an oblique approach to the subject, found that only 12 per cent of the boys and 18 per cent of

[1] Hollingshead, op. cit., p. 266.   [2] Havighurst, *et al.*, op. cit., p. 91.
[3] Ibid., p. 95.   [4] Ibid.

the girls had been to either church or Sunday school. Seventeen per
cent of the boys and 10 per cent of the girls stayed in bed until
11 a.m. or later, 17 per cent of the boys and 4 per cent of the
girls did odd jobs at home or read papers, and 15 per cent of the boys
as compared with only 1 per cent of the girls took part in sports or
played games.[1] A few did homework, rather more went for a walk,
a handful visited friends and some worked. Work in the home
associated with various domestic chores occupied no less than 42
per cent of the girls and only 3 per cent of the boys—a pointer to the
way in which youngsters at an early age are accustomed to role
differentiations based on sex.

Bryan Reed in his investigation of young people's lives in Birming-
ham towards the end of the nineteen-forties reported that under a
quarter of his young respondents were regular church attenders.[2]

In my own small study of eighty-eight dockland boys in South
Liverpool I discovered that church attendance was practically
confined to the R.C.s[3] Only 18 per cent of the Protestants, who
accounted for half the research group, attended some form of church
service and these somewhat irregularly, while 85 per cent of the
Catholics claimed to attend Mass every Sunday morning. Nevertheless, the Catholics were no less delinquent than the non-Catholics
which suggests that there is not an immediate transference of values
learned in church into the sphere of everyday conduct.

Miss Veness[4] in analysing the preoccupations of boys and girls
as evidenced in their life stories found that the girls mentioned
religion more frequently than the boys (7 per cent as contrasted
with only 1½ per cent), but unfortunately she did not collect any
information about church attendance or membership. Although
only the minority seemed to be stirred by definitely devotional
motives and to experience traditional religious aspirations, e.g. to
become or 'see' themselves as missionaries, some of their essays
were 'written in such a way as to remind us of the emotional intensity
of which adolescents become capable, once their imaginations and
their devotion have been aroused.'

M. P. Carter[5] in his book on Sheffield school leavers briefly
looked into the matter of church association in his chapter on

[1] Wilkins, op. cit., p. 92.
[2] Bryan Reed, *Eighty Thousand Adolescents*; Allen and Unwin, 1950.
[3] J. B. Mays, *Growing Up In The City*, p. 94.
[4] Veness, op. cit., pp. 104–6.   [5] Carter, op. cit.

'Leisure Activities.' Of his research group of two hundred, he found that only eleven boys and thirty-nine girls 'went to church fairly regularly at some stage during the research period,' and that only four boys and sixteen girls were regular attenders 'at all stages,' which suggests that institutionalised religion played a very small part in the lives of the majority of these young people. 'The drop in Church-going,' he thought, 'is accounted for chiefly by the readiness of parents to let their children decide for themselves after they had become workers, combined with the belief—especially amongst boys—that to go to church was a childish activity.'[1] A further reason given was that after a full working week they 'felt like a lie-in on Sunday mornings.'

Carter was of the opinion that when youngsters were members of clubs which were attached to worshipping communities they seemed to continue to attend church more regularly and for a longer period; 'about half the boys and girls who regularly went to Church at the end of the year also went to Youth Clubs or other youth organisations.' He points out, however, that church going was for many of them a social activity offering 'a chance to dress up and meet friends, as well as a means of worship.'[2]

Pearl Jephcot,[3] who studied young people in London and Nottingham in connection with a King George Jubilee Trust project, came to a conclusion which synchronises with the findings of most of the other studies we have cited. She and her fellow research workers were particularly interested in discovering if youth clubs sponsored by religious bodies did a better social job than those which were purely secular in origin. The great challenge, as they saw it, was how far church groups could cope effectively with the less favoured kind of youngsters for whom, one might have expected, their quasi-missionary spirit was eminently suitable, or, for whom they might reasonably be presumed to feel a very special responsibility to try to help. Miss Jephcot, however, came to the conclusion that 'the Church units on the whole appeared to make no more effective an attack than the secular ones on the below-average adolescents, on the bad streets, on the bottom level homes and on the delinquent-breeding areas.'[4]

The reason for this comparative failure is put down to the family background from which the youngsters come. Just, as we have seen,

---

[1] Carter, op cit., pp. 301–2.   [2] Ibid.

[3] Pearl Jephcot, *Some Young People*, Allen and Unwin, 1954.   [4] Ibid, p. 123.

failure to do well in school subjects and to pass examinations and the likelihood of attending church or being a church member are all strongly associated with the social class of the home, so, too, apparently youth work is also profoundly influenced by the same factors.[1] Not only do boys and girls from better class homes and more demanding schools make most use of the available facilities but even when these facilities are associated with and provided by an acknowledged Christian unit the final outcome is very little different. In other words, social class background and the quality of family life (the two factors are inextricably intertwined), are probably more important determinants of behaviour than specifically religious institutions. Church and Chapel, like school and club, pale into insignificance when compared with the overriding influence of home and locality. Socio-cultural factors, in the last analysis, stubbornly resist most of our orthodox religious and educational attempts to promote change. This does not mean that spiritual, moral and pedagogical institutions are necessarily ineffective; but it does seem to imply that the methods used so far to relate them creatively and positively in specific social situations have not been very successful.

Carter has already hinted at the reason why the church groups in Sheffield appeared to be successful in retaining some of the youngsters' church allegiance. It was due, he thought, to social influence and the opportunity these church clubs provided for social intercourse.

Girls seem to go to church more often than their brothers, just as in many districts they seem to be better pupils. This may be the result of some innate temperamental differences between the two sexes, but is more likely, in my view, to derive from the differential upbringing and training they receive.

The youngsters of Westminster, who under the guidance of Jordan and Fisher, became actively engaged on a study of their own locality, asked questions of some of the members of a church youth group in the district which seemed particularly well patronised. 'It was interesting,' wrote Jordan and Fisher, in their fascinating book, 'that not one of the members questioned by our team as to their reason for joining this club gave religion. Some 75 per cent cited ballroom dancing.'[2]

[1] Pearl Jephcot, op. cit., p. 128.   [2] Jordan and Fisher, op. cit., p. 75.

The respondents may, of course, have been embarrassed by the questioners. They may have felt that religious motives would have at once been suspect to other teenagers and that any answers giving religious motives for joining the church club would have been met with derision. One can never know what is in the minds of people who answer social research workers' queries, and I have no desire to build very much on the basis of the evidence cited. However, it does seem fair to deduce that social needs mainly actuate young people of all kinds and that, if these needs are being met by a youth organisation, it does not matter very much what the latter's origins and intentions are. The desire to be with one's age-mates, to do things together, is essentially what makes youngsters join and, indeed, leave many kinds of voluntary groups and there is no reason to think that those with a missionary purpose or those integrally associated with church or chapel are exempt from this rule.

It may be complained that the essense of the preceding paragraphs is to show that, whatever they do, youth groups attached to worshipping bodies cannot win. If boys and girls attend, then they do so for the wrong reasons; their motives are purely social and recreational. If they do not attend, then there is obviously something amiss. Even if it can be shown in a small number of cases that active attendance at a church youth group is associated with being a regular church attender too, this is still not regarded as enough. What do we expect church youth groups to do and achieve?

The answer to such expostulatory questions is, I think, that we expect them to do no more and no less than what they do. Youth groups, whether attached to churches or associated with entirely secular bodies, are subject to the same rules and influences. Just because they set out with certain specific purposes, e.g. to get young people to join their church or to confront them with the challenge of Christ, they need not imagine that these rules and influences are thereby magically dispelled. Young people, if they come to their clubs and youth groups, will still in the main come for the fellowship they find there and for the chance to meet and do things with their contemporaries rather than to submit themselves to spiritual influence or moral guidance. Failure to face this fact has caused considerable pain to many devout church and chapel members. There are those well-known older members of congregations who say bitterly 'We let the youngsters have our hall for badminton and other games twice a week but they don't come to the services on

Sunday any more regularly' and so on. I mention this point here because it is a very real part of the experience of any adolescent who, in search of a way of life, joins a club sponsored by a worshipping community. Instead of welcoming his arrival, the adults tend to keep him under constant surveillance and to scrutinise his activities with the most uncharitable asperity. The brutal truth is that many adults want to force young people to conform to their ideas of what is proper behaviour. They have moral intentions towards them, and, sooner or later, the majority of young people become aware of this attempted exploitation and quietly extricate themselves from the situation.

4

It will be clear from the foregoing that we ought to distinguish in our minds between several obviously related but far from identical aspects of spiritual development. First of all there are the moral principles and ethical scruples which govern individual conduct. These, we have argued, are by and large derived from traditional Christian teaching and Biblical study. Other notions, political and humanistic, also colour the contemporary climate so that idealistic ideas of the nature of justice, the proper ordering of society, the destiny of mankind are freely ventilated and discussed in newspapers, books and the market-place. There are also, today perhaps for the first time, definite materialistic and even atheistic influences at work in the world at large and in British society. People of some stature and influence publicly deny and sometimes even deride the concept of the divine. True, the attack is often launched against a debased image of God, or at least an outmoded interpretation of His Nature and Being. However that may be, youngsters nurtured more or less in orthodox religion find such challenges at times overwhelming. Students who come to a university fresh from homes and schools where at least God is honoured in name may break down emotionally when confronted with the devastating logical onslaughts of those who are intellectually their superiors. The mental and psychic disturbance can be very serious indeed for those who have never before been confronted with the paradoxes of their so-called beliefs, and very little skilled aid is available to give such unfortunate students the help and support that is needed to assist them to face up to severe intellectual challenges to what is no more than a basically juvenile and complacent faith.

Secondly, there is the whole business of being a member of a religious group or church. This can be divided into two aspects: being a member and being an attender. This could be termed the pietistic element in religious behaviour. Obviously it need not have very much connection with either the practice of coherent moral principles or with the living of a life in harmony with the spirit of Christ. It could indeed be nothing more than a shelter from reality, a refusal to face the claims of one's neighbour, a dugout for 'whited sepulchres.'[1]

There is therefore what we may call true religion; in this country almost certainly it will be true Christianity. This involves a dedicated pursuit of the good as identified and indicated in the life and teaching of the Founder. There is also bad religion which is merely the outward sign of conformity without much relation to an inward striving to be of Christ's mind. These two groups will consist of all those who are church members, sectarians, people who avow their allegiance to the religion publicly and practise it in private—a heterogeneous body of men, women and children of varying classes and social backgrounds and adhering to separatist denominations each of which cleaves to its own individual interpretation of 'the truth.' We may estimate their number as no more than a quarter of the population with perhaps rather more young people under the age of fourteen than between the ages of fourteen and twenty-one or so. This accounts for those children who attend Sunday schools of one sort or another during their childhood but leave it behind on the threshold of adolescence and never move on into any adult worshipping community. This, as we have already seen, is to a considerable extent due to the fact that their parents are not themselves church or chapel members. Lacking parental example and support at this stage they very easily succumb to the temptations of the peer group to drift away from organised religion and to regard everything associated with it as 'soft,' 'sissy' or 'kids' stuff'. As various studies have shown, in households unattached to any church or denomination, the drift away from religious practices is most noticeable.[2]

---

[1] Cf. G. J. Renier's remark: 'It is easier to observe the Sabbath than to love one's neighbour', *The English Are They Human?*; Benn, 1931, p. 227.

[2] Miss Jean Hill's study of Liverpool school leavers, already referred to, for example, also brings this fact out clearly. Her evidence in the main suggests that

Finally, there is that great majority of people, young and older, who would not call themselves church members, but some of whom might, if cornered, confess themselves to be Christians, many of whom believe in some sort of a God and have hazy notions of an after-life. I suspect that there are a great number of folk in our society like this; not irreligious or anti-church, faintly coloured by memories of Christian ethical teaching, but vague, unattached, drifters between the devout past and an irreligious future. They are not to be confused with that small, selective group of 'seekers after truth,' intellectuals and others who are dissatisfied with formal religion, cannot accept most of the dogmatic teaching of the churches, cannot indeed give allegiance to the idea of a personal Creator Spirit at all but who, nevertheless, live scrupulous lives and submit their consciences to moral principles. Many of this small group would call themselves humanists. A few derive their moral ideas from the study of science which it is claimed is not ethically neutral but 'by itself is able to provide mankind with a way of life which is firstly, self-consistent and harmonious, and secondly, free for the exercise of that objective reason on which our material progress depends.'[1]

Other humanists claim to base their moral standards on principles which are either derived directly from or are very closely harmonious with Christianity. They eschew the metaphysics, they find the theology unacceptable, but nevertheless wholeheartedly approve the Christian moral code as they understand it. It is often said by the formally religious and the devout that such an attitude is merely parasitic upon the tree of Christian faith, that it owes its strength to the religion it no longer espouses and disowns and dishonours its parentage. For these reasons, it is argued by the orthodox, it can at best be a passing phase. If formal religion and organised Christianity were to perish, this Christian humanism would in time perish also. I cannot myself accept this judgement as valid or see why, in the end, a kind of 'religionless' Christianity, of the kind that has recently been under discussion by theologians and others, should not prevail.[2]

church attendance with one or the other parent is an important factor in the child's continued attendance at church, especially in the case of those who have been educated at denominational schools.

[1] C. H. Waddington, *The Scientific Attitude*, Penguin Books, revised edition, 1948, p. 170. The author puts forward the idea that science is man's true religion, not as a supernatural gift but as the necessary moral ground of our being to carry on our evolution as a species.

[2] Cf. Dietrich Bonhoeffer, *Letters and Papers From Prison*, S.C.M. Press, 1953; Fontana Books, 1959.

The argument here, however, is not so much concerned with the small group of religious doubters actively concerned with the discovery of 'truth' (whatever that might signify) as with the majority of young people outside the church, as we know them to be, and the moral values and religious ideas they may or may not develop and demonstrate. We might usefully conclude this chapter by pointing out that, on the basis of the admittedly scanty evidence assembled, young people are on the whole more often than not inclined to be spiritually adrift or certainly rather hazy about their doctrinal beliefs and philosophical position generally. They have ethical values, mainly derived from the Hebraic and Christian traditions, but only lukewarmly put them into practice. If they go to church or chapel it is as often as not for what the devout would term purely secular reasons. They go, that is to say, for human fellowship rather than for Holy Communion. Class interests and influences largely condition religious ideas and practices, those whose families are doing fairly well in a worldly sense tending to be more likely to be linked to a church than those whose families are social failures or who are definitely lower down in the social order—although one would want to make an important exception here in the case of Roman Catholics who not only tend to be members of low income and status groups but also more regular practitioners of their religious obligations than non-Catholics.

Youth as a whole, however, is not strikingly committed to either a religious way of life or to active concern with moral and social issues. The minority again—usually intellectuals and products of serious-minded homes—are, but the great majority seem to be much more concerned with getting a good job with financial prospects and in some intrinsically interesting field than with the pursuit of the good life as interpreted by moral philosophers. This is not said in critical disparagement. Far from it. There is a healthy scepticism amongst many teenagers and a rejection of sham values and shoddy hypocritical professions of faith which augers well for their own and society's future. Above all, perhaps, the 'true religion' of the young is bound up with their deep concern for the human personality and for the right kind of human relationships. This, as already stated in an earlier section, is a reassuring fact. To quote E. M. Eppel:

When one looks more closely at the kind of conditions which are stressed by these young workers, it is clear that there is a considerable concern for good human relations and a resentment of authoritarianism.

The dominant attitude is summed up in the declaration of one 17 year old: "They should put themselves in the place of the person to whom they give the order. . . . An order can be made into a friendly gesture by asking a person to do something."[1]

Thus, it is on the quality of human relationships of every kind and in any situation, at school, at work or leisure, that they are apt to judge the rightness or the wrongness of any particular action, rather than in terms of abstract moral or religious principles.

There is obviously nothing like a moral landslide amongst the rising generation. There may be some grounds for criticising youth —hedonism, fecklessness, lack of ambition, complacency—but their 'rejection of a legalistic morality is very far from being a sign of decadence'[2] in itself. Our conclusion must surely be with Professor Mace, who, summing up the significance of the Birkbeck College students' survey, said it should serve as a corrective to sensational and alarmist reports on juvenile delinquency and the moral laxity of the young, rather than with the latterday Jeremiahs.

We just do not know how many of our boys had coshed, or were later to cosh, old ladies. We just do not know how many of our schoolgirls carried contraceptives in their handbags. We do not know even how many of these boys and girls were cigarette addicts. It was not that kind of research. What we think we do know is that whatever our dreadful boys did, and whatever our girls carried in their handbags, there was in all of them a streak of decency and serious mindedness, some evidence of purpose in life.[3]

And more than that we have perhaps no right to expect, although we may hope for better things to come.

[1] Eppel, op. cit.

[2] Dr Eustace Chesser in *Teenage Morals*, An Education Pamphlet, 1961, p. 16.

[3] Veness, op. cit.

Part Three

Part Three

In preceding chapters we have discussed the role and status of the adolescent in contemporary society from both theoretical and research angles. We have examined the contributions of various empirical studies and we have also taken cognizance of some broad hypotheses about the nature and function of adolescence in mainly sociological terms. While there may be nothing like unanimity on the part of the various 'authorities' quoted, there nevertheless appears to be widespread agreement on one basic fact—which is that the maturational and social phase which we call youth presents social problems which it would be merely foolish to deny or under-rate.

We have seen, however, that the so-called youth problem is not confined to young people and that it is intimately associated with the whole life of the community. It arises from ordinary social processes and trends in contemporary western civilisation and cannot be evaluated in isolation. We live in a highly complex society, subject to strong pressures and influenced very often by impersonal forces which we neither perceive nor control nor understand. The result is that the vast majority of us are merely bewildered at what is happening.

Parents and other adults perceive youthful behaviour as different and hence to some degree threatening. They tend to exaggerate these differences to the point of alienation. Each instance of youthful failure to conform to the adults' expectations or hopes or rigid concepts of propriety is interpreted as a malevolent deviation to be fought and exterminated. The very word which we frequently use to categorise young people, 'teenager,' is one heavily weighted with pejorative connotations. The cleavage between the generations, because it involves inability and refusal to accept and comprehend necessary differences, could be called a state of cultural *anomie*. In so far as this is true it is a threat to the stability of the social structure. If teachers do not understand their charges, if parents are irritated and angered by their children's attitudes and behaviour, much social damage must inevitably accrue.

Two things stand out in relation to the 'youth problem.' First, it is crosscultural and universal. All Western societies seem to be afflicted with the same kind of problems and misunderstandings. Secondly, the degree with which certain disaffected sections of young people repudiate their elders and adult culture generally is today outstandingly aggressive and flamboyant. Some psychologists seem to regard this as a 'natural' state of affairs arising as much from the adults' envy of youth as from anything intrinsically disturbed in the latter's behaviour. But we clearly cannot leave it at that. Many adults and parents are genuinely puzzled and anxious. They don't know what to do for the best, and—the other side of the coin— many youngsters too are unhappy.

The charges brought against youth are many and various. They cannot all be denied or whittled down, but those who wish to defend youth can point out, with telling logic, that these things are no more characteristic of youth than of other sections of the population. Young and older people are equally affected to some degree or another. In fact, as far as some of the charges on the indictment go, teenagers clearly have a better record than other age groups. One thing, at least, to be said for many young men and women today is that, whatever their behaviour, they are frank and open about it. They neither pretend to be what they are not nor do they wallow in confessional emotionalism. We may not always approve of what the Arthur Seatons do or admire their motivation. But there is often something rugged and independent about them which we cannot help liking and responding to positively. Little good will come either from adopting a mainly critical or an entirely defensive position. Degrees of culpability can be left for the future to determine and apportion.

Sufficient evidence is available to show that a fair sized group of young people do not make a success of their lives in the conditions of today. The River City enquiry suggested that this might be well over a quarter of the age group. It is precisely with these youngsters who fail to fit in and make a go of their lives in terms of prevailing adult norms that we ought to be deeply concerned—not be it said, with the idea of making them conformist and subservient but simply because of the ordinary individual's natural right to happiness and security. Repudiation of established customs is not always undesirable nor necessarily pathological. A degree of protest behaviour can be accepted as healthy. But we have to count the cost to the protesters themselves, and this is a point that is often overlooked. The widely disseminated stereotype of the tough Teddy Boy gang is, as

Peter Scott[1] amongst others has shown, largely fictional. The vast majority, even of violent and aggressive young delinquents, are inadequate and rather pathetic personalities whose ultimate prognosis is not necessarily bad provided that they are wisely and lovingly handled.

We ought to be much more concerned really about the less dramatic but often more far-reaching consequences of the differences and misunderstandings between the two generations and age groups —the quiet distrust, the stubborn incomprehension, the mutual intransigence which leads to a state of cold war between teacher and pupil, parent and child. The fact may well be that today the gap is widening, the psychological gulf is going deeper. It is a process which once set under way may prove very difficult to counteract.

It may well be that in the past we exaggerated the level of general morality but at least there was an acceptance of the idea that standards existed. Now, apparently, fashions in conduct as in clothes style rule the day.

Sociologists point to the failure of our society to give adolescents a real enough role to play in its affairs. Kingsley Davis suggests that it is 'ennui' as much as anything else that drives the youngster 'to participate in a more vivid world, the world of youth culture.'[2] School, home, society as a whole fail to satisfy his interests at this climacteric with the result that he escapes into irresponsibility, interpreted as 'having a good time' in the spheres of athletics and sex. Adolescence in our culture is allocated 'no avowed function in the institutional structure but is interstitial, officially purposeless —a phenomenon seldom found in other societies.'[3]

The adolescent, then, is a marginal figure, having much in common with coloured people, and other despised minorities. He reacts to his marginality by retreating into an unreal world of pleasure. Friedenberg has carried this kind of analysis to its extreme conclusion in his study of what he termed 'The Vanishing Adolescent.' To Friedenberg adolescence is much more than a physical process, more indeed than the mere attainment of sexual maturity, it is for him 'primarily a social process, whose fundamental task is clear and stable self-identification.'[4]

[1] Scott, op. cit. See pp. 28–30 above.
[2] Kingsley Davis, *Human Society*; Macmillan, 12th printing, 1959, p. 227.
[3] Ibid., pp. 227–28.
[4] Edgar Z. Friedenberg, op. cit.

Thus any retreat into sheer banality, into an irresponsible pursuit of pleasure is a failure to be a true adolescent. We are all of us to some extent to blame for the cult of banality in modern youth in that we acquiesce in their economic exploitation by those firms which have expressly set out to stimulate and satisfy young people's demands for particular kinds of consumer goods and entertainments. Even teenage defiance of a more flamboyant sort is, as David Matza has pointed out, encouraged by elements in the adult community. What he calls the 'subterranean traditions' in respectable society stimulate and derive satisfaction from youthful excesses. Contemporary culture, indeed, has the effect, Friedenberg argues, of producing pliability to such a degree that adolescence becomes more and more hazardous and thus 'fewer youngsters dare to go through with it; they merely undergo puberty and simulate maturity.'[1] 'True' adolescence, the search for the valid self-image, is swallowed up and consumed in a spurious precocity. The fully human adolescent in fact is the one who gives trouble to himself and to the community. That is the nature of adolescence, to face life 'with love and defiance.' Excess conformity of an other-directed kind destroys, or, at least, inhibits the authentic spirit of youth from revealing itself. The self cannot then emerge via the process of differentiation at all. Individuality is stifled and true personality muffled in an atmosphere of general 'blandness' and superficiality. In Friedenberg's view the adolescent ought to rebel. Indeed he says 'adolescence *is* conflict—protracted conflict between the individual and society,' and it is only by conflict that 'an individual learns the complex, subtle, and precious difference between himself and his environment.' In a world of organisation men, fully grown or maturing, 'a society in which there is no difference or in which no difference is permitted, the word "adolescence" has no meaning.'[2]

We are led, therefore, to a point of some disagreement. Some critics of contemporary youth express alarm at the exaggerated manner of their repudiation of adult values and standards. Others, like Friedenberg, are concerned that there is insufficient adolescent rebellion for social health. Which is the truer analysis? Is there too much conformity or excess rebellion?

As we have constantly stressed throughout the text, at the moment we have too little evidence to answer these questions with any degree of scientific accuracy. The various researches which we have quoted

[1] Edgar Z. Friedenberg, op. cit., p. 17.   [2] Ibid., p. 34.

from and our own personal experiences and observations suggest that both these views are to some extent correct. They are correct as far as they go, but ultimately misleading and partial. They are misleading, I believe, because of the familiar failure to discriminate between different kinds of people when making general statements. The generalisations of individual psychologists or sociologists cannot be made to refer to the entire age range and to members of each and every social class or status group. What we have to do here, by way of summarising much of the available material, is to indicate the bounds within which these generalisations seem to be valid. To this end I now offer a very rough and ready typology of adolescents in which I have tried to take into account various social class and subcultural differences.

Group I. This comprises those youngsters who react aggressively against the limitations of their environment. They may to some extent have been denied the requisite support and affection at home at a crucial stage of their development, but they are also products of an inadequate educational system which has failed to fit them for the kind of work which is socially well esteemed and financially highly rewarded. They are the young people who, in terms of Robert K. Merton's analysis, find themselves socially frustrated in the effort to attain the goals which are culturally prescribed in their particular society.[1] In a society which greatly stresses the importance of success as measured by making money they are the ones who tend to be written off as failures and misfits.

The young people in this group are by definition lower class and low status. Their protest takes the form of hostility towards 're-spectable' society and its institutions. Their subculture also embodies certain compensatory elements in so far as individuals achieve status and exhibit prowess within it and, in terms of their own goals, they may become successful, well-adjusted people. They are the 'roughs,' the 'toughs' and what is usually meant by the loose generic title of 'Teddy Boys.'

Group II. This consists of a similar socially depressed and unsuccessful stratum which does not, however, react by open aggression against the 'respectables' but contents itself with participation in certain illegal practices and rackets such as gambling and some forms of political corruption. Young people in this group may be thought

[1] Robert K. Merton, *Social Theory and Social Structure*; The Free Press, Revised edition, 1957, pp. 161–94.

of as socially well-adjusted both in relation to their equals and to the culture of the wider society. They avoid violence yet they are not retreatist. The type is admirably described by William Foote Whyte in his classic study of 'corner boys' in Boston.[1]

Group III. This is made up of the 'beats,' 'queers' and other socially and psychologically depressed elements. Their reaction is one of withdrawal. Often they seek escape via drugs and alcohol or by the espousal of some world-rejecting religion. They are basically inadequate types and wish to withdraw into their own world of similarly minded people. Some are sexual deviants and some become prostitutes and others exist on the shadowy fringe of social life.

Group IV. These are the Angry Young Men or rather, nowadays, their descendants. They are politically leftish, strongly humanitarian in their attitude and emotionally extremely sore and sensitive. They are often well-educated and eagerly adopt such causes as anti-apartheid or support the activities of the Committee of 100 and similar campaigns for nuclear disarmament. They seem to comprise members of most income groups and to represent a considered attitude of mind rather than a class-conditioned prejudice.

Group V. These are the new men of the affluent society, the new type of proletarian male especially, cast in the Arthur Seaton mould. They are working class in origin and background but view the world optimistically and pugnaciously. They have good skilled work, high wages and in the main are highly satisfied with themselves. They enjoy the physical and material good things of life; clothes, money, cars, sex. They seem to suffer from few inhibitions and not to be burdened by too many scruples. They are perhaps rather brash, banal yet remarkably likeable types.

Group VI. This is made up of the middle class grammar/public and high school battalions who have made a good adjustment to the realities of life in their milieux and accept its goals and aspirations. They mean to do well in school, to pass their examinations and qualify themselves for good professional or commercial employment. Many go to universities. The upper echelons become top business executives and managers. In a sense they epitomise the values which contemporary society promotes and rewards.

Like any typology, the above is open to many criticisms. For one

[1] William Foote Whyte, *Street Corner Society*; University of Chicago Press, revised edition, 1955.

thing there must obviously be considerable overlapping between the main groups as outlined. Very many individuals, moreover, will not easily be placed in any of the categories without reservations being made. Nevertheless, as a broad generalisation I think it probably holds good and can at least form the basis for discussion and further research.

The majority of young people will clearly be found in Groups V and VI, while Groups I to IV contain most of those deemed by conventional society to be deviants or failures. It is the latter, however, who receive most of the publicity and it is they, too, who, in the main, have given to the word 'teenager' a somewhat pejorative flavour. We have to beware, of course, of labelling a perfectly normal youngster who is going through an unconventional or rebelliously bohemian phase as a true deviant. It is well to remind ourselves once again that the great majority of young people are comparatively passive and conformist, often to the point of dull mediocrity. Perhaps the brightest and more interesting youngsters are those who, while generally accepting the values of the community into which they are born, nevertheless evidence some degree of protest and criticism and so offer a challenge to the establishment. They probably comprise the future leaders of society, the brighter sparks from which the future will draw its warmth and dynamism. They may be the ones who, in the ultimate analysis, will justify our concept of democracy to history.[1]

---

[1] I have perhaps tended to overlook that proportion of less successful lower class youngsters who accept their lowly status with equanimity. To some extent they will be found in my Group II but not entirely so. Perhaps they could be regarded as a sub-group of II. In any case, we may hope that their numbers will be on the decline as they comprise a group which, in the last analysis, we could very well do without.

Hitherto, although the emphasis has generally been upon the
nature of the youth culture in Britain, many comparisons have been
made with American society and frequent quotations have been
made from the comparatively richer documentation of adolescence
in transatlantic sociological literature. It is perhaps worth while
pausing at this stage to make these comparisons more explicit and
to point out also the contrasts between the ways of life in the two
countries with a view to assessing what consequences these differences may have for the future development of British society.

Although American culture clearly derives from the same basic
source as British and is an offshoot of the parent European tradition,
it has branched out in a number of highly individualistic and
distinctive ways. The idea of an open society based on free economic
enterprise rewarding the adventurous, the talented and the vigorous
is an essential element in what has come to be universally known as
'the American dream.' It is, in theory at least, a country where
achieved rather than ascribed social status is conferred on individuals
as a reward for their own exertions. Britain, on the other hand, has
moved much more slowly and cautiously along the road to egalitarianism. It has stubbornly retained the remnants of the aristocracy
and the élite of the court circle gathered by selection and the ranking
of birth and breeding around a constitutional monarchy. Its class
system, although modified and permeable, is fairly widely accepted,
even, it seems, by those who come at the bottom of the social
hierarchy.

The British educational system, moreover, seems to be much less
open than the American system of schooling in several ways.
Although both are clearly subjected to powerful class pressures
and influences, in the U.S.A. it is by no means uncommon for the
children from nearly all local families to begin their education side
by side at the local primary school. Furthermore, in America both
the co-educational and comprehensive ideas have been widely
accepted in principle and in practice. Differences and inequalities,
of course, occur all the way through the educational process, but in
America there is at least a semblance of equality and democracy at

the beginning. In Britain, by contrast, this is much less apparent. Professional and upper class parents very rarely make use of the state schools, preferring to send their children to private primary and preparatory schools before their ultimate translation to an expensive boarding establishment at the age of thirteen, and often much earlier.

All the indications suggest, in fact, that in Britain this tendency towards exclusiveness is likely to continue unabated in the future, with inevitable consequences in the way of the reinforcement of class distinctions and associated misunderstanding. The fact that something like a third of the adolescent population in the U.S.A. proceeds to some kind of fulltime higher education, as compared to the mere handful of 8 per cent or so in Britain, further illustrates the general disparity between the two countries in terms of actual opportunities available for average young citizens to achieve success in life.

The highly traditionalised nature of British society moreover still makes it possible for individuals to ascribe some of the blame for their failure to achieve to the operation of the social system rather than to any inherent deficiencies within themselves. There is some comfort in this kind of acceptance of limiting factors which makes it much less necessary in Britain for people to strive for upward social mobility.

Furthermore, the concept of welfare and the idea of the guaranteed minimum standard of living for all is much more firmly rooted in the soil of British culture than it is in the United States, where extreme poverty in certain sectors, amongst 'the dollar poor' for instance, is still tolerated by the wealthiest country in the world. Although the idea of welfare is making some headway in American society and social services are on the increase, the process has nothing like the majority support that it has in Britain, nor are there many signs that a Welfare State on the British pattern is very attractive to the average American citizen. Thus both the need for self assertion in order to prosper and reliance upon individual effort in order to survive are more marked in American as compared with British culture. In so far as this is true of great numbers of British citizens, it must make for a fairly orderly and conservatively-based social structure whose central institutions are regarded as almost sacrosanct by the majority. Thus, while British society stresses orderliness and limited aspiration and is characterised by an astonishing degree of tough stability, American society, with its emphasis on progress and individualism and unlimited aspiration, is by comparison much more pluralistic and less highly integrated. Its greater size, larger and more ethnically varied population, richer resources and sudden accession to pre-eminence as a world power (at a time when Britain has been obliged to accept a reduced international status) and its continuing almost fanatical adherence to a belief in the virtues of economic individualism and freedom of action have each, in their separate ways, contributed to produce a culture which, by and large, presents young people with a bewildering profusion of choices, and, what is more burdensome, a lack of secure models on which to fashion their own development. Risks have to be taken and wrong choices are often made. A certain degree of socially induced anxiety is therefore an inevitable by-product of the functioning of the American social system. In Britain the tension and anxiety are considerably lessened and social roles are both more limited and rather more clearly defined and predetermined. It is a difference of degree rather than of kind, but the social problems resulting from the amount of frustration and tension are obviously much less serious and less widespread in Britain than they are in the United States. The response of a great many American youngsters to their indeterminate social role has been to create a youth culture as something almost entirely apart from the rest of the community's life—a kind of chrysalis phase between childhood and maturity with its own system of values and associated behavioural norms. This phase is seen not so much as a preparation for maturity (although it is to some extent this, too) as a protest against the rejecting adult world and a defensive mechanism against isolation and misunderstanding. At its most extreme position this defensiveness passes over to the attack and becomes openly hostile and aggressive, and in its deviant and parapathological manifestations becomes strongly rebellious and criminalistic.

The Beatnik phenomenon of withdrawal from normal society originated in America and has never made much inroad into British youth culture. One of the reasons for this may well be that Britain, unlike America, has not in recent years wallowed in a floodtide of material prosperity against which young people felt obliged to protest in such a dramatic manner. All the manifestations of youthful intransigence in fact seem to be much more clearly visible in

American society than in the less expansive and more tradition-bound culture of Britain.

Thus to a greater extent in the United States status aspirations and insecurities centring around the fulfilment of prescribed social roles can be used to account for teenage hegemony on the one hand and for delinquency on the other. Although it has sometimes been suggested by theorists like Cohen[1] that social frustration and allied anxieties, and consequent misbehaviour, can only be used to account for the delinquencies of working class and underprivileged youth, there have been recent attempts to show that middle class delinquency may be similarly associated with the same kind of frustrations and fears.[2] Cohen thought that middle class 'bad' behaviour must be largely due to what has been called the 'masculine protest' against an upbringing and home life overshadowed by the mother's emotional influence and the associated danger of feminine identification. Delinquent and rebellious acts on the part of a middle class American boy, then, are seen as an attempt to reassure himself of his own manliness, as a kind of 'proving' activity, a substitute perhaps for the *rites of passage* and the initiating ceremonies into adult life practised by more primitive communities. Sexual delinquency obviously fits very neatly in with this kind of analysis. But there are serious objections to the wholesale acceptance of this masculine protest explanation, the chief of which centres on the known statistical fact that there is less middle class than lower class delinquency.[3] In Britain this regularity is very clearly marked indeed, and whatever ways one tries to juggle with the official crime figures, it is impossible to deny the fact that, by and large, juvenile crime is a proletarian activity. In America, although the same regularity has been observed over the generations, there have been indications recently that the differentials between the classes are being reduced. Several writers, for example, have put forward the tentative notion that middle class delinquency is actually on the increase.[4] The evidence for this is as yet extremely shaky, but if it should prove to be so then here is yet another divergence from the British pattern.

[1] Cohen, op. cit.

[2] Cf. M. Gold, *Status Forces in Delinquent Boys*; Institute for Social Research, University of Michigan, 1963.

[3] This has been challenged by some American writers but, in my judgment, unsuccessfully.

[4] Cf. Robert H. Bohlke, 'Social Mobility, Stratification Inconsistency and Middle Class Delinquency', *Social Problems*, vol. viii, No. 4, 1961.

The balance of professional opinion is still unclear. Gold,[1] for example, has suggested that middle class American boys commit offences and misbehave because they are fundamentally insecure about their status and achievements, although, since their chances of actually experiencing failure are much less than for working class youth, the proportion who actually break the law or who deviate in other ways is very much reduced in their case. In Gold's view, delinquency is the ideal solution for status problems for all social classes and groups because, as Cohen[2] has indicated, it simultaneously cocks a firm snook at frustrating society and offers opportunities for gaining a substitute kind of high status amongst the serried ranks of fellow dissidents.

The actual situation is, in my view however, likely to be much less clear cut than either Gold or Cohen suppose. I am inclined to regard the Cohen hypothesis as only a partial explanation of juvenile delinquency even in American society. Some evidence has come in in recent years to question the reality of the social protest element on which Cohen's analysis depends and to substitute instead the idea that working class boys, by and large, accept middle class norms as legitimate but behave themselves in ways which are essentially self-defeating in relation to the middle class goals which they feel incapable of achieving. Furthermore, the argument put forward by Walter Miller in America and by Morris and myself in Britain suggests that there is something in the nature of lower class culture itself which incorporates a limited amount of criminal behaviour as part and parcel of a way of life which exists in its own right and not merely as a form of reaction against frustrated social ambitions.[3] As far as the evidence in British studies is concerned, it seems likely that there exists a fundamental difference in aspiration between middle and lower class families, and it is reasonable to suppose that this is itself associated with a rather more stable and less open kind of social system than operates in the U.S.A.

[1] Gold, op. cit.   [2] Cohen, op. cit.

[3] Walter B. Miller, 'Lower Class Culture as a Generating Milieu of Gang Delinquency', *Journal of Social Issues*, vol. 14 (1958), No. 3; T. Morris, *The Criminal Area*, Routledge and Kegan Paul, 1957; J. B. Mays, *Growing Up in the City*, Liverpool University Press, 1954, and John Wiley Science Editions, 1964. David J. Bordua's paper 'Delinquent Subcultures: Sociological Interpretations of Gang Delinquency', *Annals*, November 1961, *Teenage Culture*, pp. 119–36, is a most interesting discussion of the whole topic.

The preceding paragraphs may suggest that both America and Britain are essentially and ineradicably pathogenic societies. This view would be quite erroneous. It is always dangerous to exaggerate discontinuities between youth and the rest of the community, and perhaps our modern concern with deviants and delinquents has tended to lead us into this kind of error. For the youth cult is also subtly connected with adult culture, as Matza has shown, and thus the cleavage between adolescence and maturity is not so fundamental as superficial impressions might suggest. The worship of the scholar-athlete in American high schools emphasises this kind of general conformity of outlook between older and younger generations, for the scholar-athlete is also the paragon of parents and the ideal of pedagogues. The fact that as far as the middle class youngsters go they mostly adore the scholar-athlete as someone who is also highly successful in love affairs and in sexual relations ought not to blind us to the fact of the underlying consensus between the age-groups. The cult has, of course, a more universal base than may generally be supposed. Its origins undoubtedly go back to the cultural foundations of European civilisation and more especially to Athenian society in pre-Christian times. But it is also an ideal which has strong links with middle class educational culture in Britain, where for a long time now the scholar-athlete has been the acme of public school achievement, although the British scholar-athlete, while perhaps less successful in his amours, is expected to pack a pretty stiff dose of ethical strenuousness and high moral enthusiasm which his American counterpart is spared.

In speaking about delinquents or social misfits in both societies we are still talking about minorities, however, although as far as the United States is concerned, the proportion of misfits and malcontents is clearly much in excess of Britain. Both countries face problems of over as well as of under conformity. Both countries produce large numbers of nondescript individuals who shake down fairly satisfactorily into the existing conditions. The proportion of young people in American society who are seen to be cut off from the main cultural stream is almost certainly much larger than in Britain and crime and deviant problems are much severer in the former. The implications of the River City study point unmistakably in this direction, although the findings of the Newsom Committee suggest that similar if milder problems face British administrators too. American schools face the severe problems of the so-called 'dropouts' ('early leavers' in Britain) and a consequent much higher rate of youthful unemployment than England has experienced since the nineteen-thirties.

Frank Riessman in his book, *The Culturally Deprived Child*,[1] has highlighted this grave problem and estimates that by 1970 one in every two youngsters in the larger American cities will be educationally underprivileged. In his interesting monograph, which has obvious applicability for British conditions also, he suggests, however, that middle class educators have tended to exaggerate ths resistance to educational influences on the part of lower class children. He advances some good reasons for believing that the failure of such children in school is as much due to poor teaching methods as to any fundamental incompatibility between deprived pupils and the goals of the central culture. The schools and the educational process itself is pervaded by strong and subtle biases in favour of middle and against lower class children.

Both societies have enjoyed an era of comparatively greater affluence. Young people in America are, of course, very much richer in actual spending power than their counterparts in Britain. American teenage culture is itself the product of affluence in an expanding economy which 'can afford a large leisure class of youngsters not in the labour force but yet consumers on a vast scale, or, if in the labour force, free to spend their earnings on themselves'[2]—a phenomenon which has emerged in recent years and which is hitherto unknown in western history. In Britain, although the same influences are at work, we still look upon adolescents as producers as well as consumers of wealth. What they earn in Britain is open to the same kind of economic exploitation as in America. In Britain too the pop star has soared into the ascendant and, following the transatlantic lead, we are busy in the creation of a new kind of sub-cultural royalty, of which perhaps the Beatles are a prototype. The sexual *mores* of young people in both countries are topics of widespread concern. Premarital intercourse and promiscuity is a public debating point in London as in New York. Although the institution of 'dating' has not caught on in Britain, it is obvious that earlier sex experience and greater mingling between the sexes is on the increase. One of the forces in British society which is at the moment acting as a bulwark against a more sexually open kind of youth

[1] Frank Riessman, *The Culturally Deprived Child*, Harper and Row, New York, 1962.   [2] Bernard, op. cit., p. 3.

culture is our long-established tradition of monosexual schooling. The attitudes and behaviour of teenagers in American high schools is delayed somewhat in Britain and found in evidence at university rather than at grammar school level. But apart from the temporal lag, the pattern of relationships is broadly very similar.

British culture remains under fire from American films, television programmes and literature. Will Britain in another thirty years or so resemble present-day America? The same kind of political apathy has been described by critics of youth on both sides of the Atlantic. Nostrums and ameliorative prescriptions, such as the American Peace Corps, have been discussed in Britain in recent months, and for more or less the same reasons. Affluence and an easier mode of life have brought associated problems of drift into banality. Behind the external glitter of a rising standard of living the same signs of inner unease have been observed as a threat to the future. 'In many respects,' concluded Michael Banton in his monograph which compared the role of the police officer in Britain and America, 'our social organisation is coming to resemble that of the United States, and many of the problems that have appeared there may be expected here.'[1]

One of the factors which will exert a crucial effect on the future of British society is her capacity for economic growth. If she falls substantially behind other European countries in productivity and fails to develop along the lines which have already brought riches to America, many of the features and problems which afflict contemporary U.S.A. could remain marginal and fractional in Britain. A new and less affluent way of life may become an inevitability which British people will be obliged to accept and perhaps it will turn out in the end to be a not entirely undesirable state of affairs.

---

[1] M. Banton, *The Policeman in the Community*, Tavistock Publications, London, 1964, p. 261.

CHAPTER VIII

FURTHER ASPECTS AND SUGGESTIONS

1

The problems of youth are not likely to prove amenable to the application of any simple nostrums and it would be a bold man indeed who would suggest new measures to cope with them in any spirit of dogmatic self-assurance. There are, however, a number of things that we might do to help to reduce the tensions inherent in the situation and to contain the problem within manageable proportions.

But before going on to suggest what practical steps could be taken it is important to stress the fact that the problems of youth should be understood and treated only within the framework of society as a whole. The difficulties which many young people seem to experience in establishing themselves in the world depend partly on their own make-up and attitudes and partly, also, on the social situation within which they are obliged to operate. No long term easement of their difficulties is likely to take place until we have succeeded in bringing about certain structural changes in our society so that our general social ends may be more readily achieved.

These ends are, in a nutshell, to create a community in which care for persons is both explicitly and implicitly promoted and fostered. The society we wish to see brought about will be one in which concern for people will be actively encouraged and not institutionally or structurally hindered. It will be an open society in the fullest possible sense. It will be open to the fullest development of every individual talent and, at the same time, it will possess the true openness of man to man, mind to mind in altruistic love and personal concern.

We are committed, in this view, to what Dr Wall calls 'the task of Constructive Education,'[1] the task of recreating our culture, using the widest possible connotation of that word, so that the ethical principles implicit in our civilisation shall be liberated and become socially dynamic.

This constructive education, it will be obvious, cannot take place unless there is a fairly widespread agreement at the moral and

[1] Wall, *Child of Our Times*, op. cit., especially pp. 83–107.

philosophical level. It is the task of all to reach such a consensus. Religious, political and ethical values will influence the final outcome in so far as there is already in existence a profound tradition of civilisation in the Western world. But each citizen must make these values his own before they can become institutionally realised. Personal decision and personal commitment cannot be avoided if we are to experience the fullness of a free and responsible society. This is a truth that must be hammered home to each and every member of the community all the time. If persons count at the ethical level, they are equally crucial at the structural and institutional level. Individual men have to make the necessary decisions to change the laws and create new formal relationships before any great advance becomes possible. If we all dither on the touch lines, the game is never started.

The task of education in the broadest sense is to promote guided social change. To some extent this concerns the discovery of new techniques and methods so that the job may be done more effectively. New kinds of schools, for example, may be necessary in order to realise communally some of the ethical values we have espoused on other grounds. The great strength of the comprehensive school lies, not in any claim that it makes teaching more effective but in its demonstration, at organisational level, of the ethical values we say we believe in. It may or may not produce the best scholars but at least it witnesses to a widespread egalitarian spirit, which may, in the last analysis, be a more important social end.

The redirection of education will also be concerned with the nature and content of the training we give young people and this is most obviously closely connected with our general values and social philosophy. Moreover, the actual procedures we employ will have a vital bearing on the outcome of our efforts. Broad notions such as 'citizenship' will not be very helpful unless we are clear what kind of a *civitas* we have in view. Children cannot be trained correctly merely by being submitted without guidance to raw experiences. Co-operation is not automatically learned by associating with others in the attempt to perform a common task. This may lead, just as easily, to a breakdown of relationships and a withdrawal into anarchy. It is essential that there shall always be at hand teachers, guides, instructors whose task will be, in part, to interpret experience to their pupils, and whose responsibility will extend, in certain circumstances, to the issuing of general directives. Teachers have the constant task of interpreting their pupils' own behaviour to themselves. They also have, what is no less a responsibility, the task of trying to live up to the ideas and values which they are offering. Education is simultaneously an influence, a demonstration *and* rational instruction. It is important not to lose sight of any of these aspects if we wish to make the maximum impression and to achieve long term results.

The procedures followed in the educational process, therefore, be it formal or informal, require that children shall have direct experience of responsibility and community life of a specific character.

If we want youngsters to be co-operative and concerned with one another's welfare to the extent of regarding the other person's wellbeing at least as of equal importance with their own, then they must be given experiences of this sort at school and in the home.[1] Moreover, their teachers and parents must set this sort of example to them and, at the same time, rational instruction must reinforce the same principles.

What holds for formal education in school and for home life, holds equally for informal education and for the Youth Service. The leisure time groups which youngsters join must offer them similar experiences of collaborative and concerned community living and set before them the same broad ethical principles which underpin the whole of civilisation.

At the present time, it must be admitted, there is often dichotomy between the principles taught and the practices carried out in our educational institutions. Religion has degenerated into a subject on the syllabus instead of being the life of the school manifest in every aspect of its affairs. At the same time the school avoids politics like the plague. Thus, in default of religion and politics, there is nothing left to give the educational process its dynamic other than egotism. Enlightened, and often very unenlightened, selfishness is all too often the ethos of the entire educational process. There is in fact no other dynamism to keep the institution going. Deprived of the great emotive forces which activate the human spirit, the whole educational business degenerates into a sordid scramble for individual awards and a squalid competitiveness between rival organisations.

---

[1] N.B. The challenge involved in the extra year of formal schooling promised as from 1970 in Britain is substantially a challenge to teachers to make their syllabus and approach relevant to the needs of those who have little interest in higher education but whose personal problems are acute.

Competitiveness between persons is surely always a deleterious condition. Those who most laud the virtues of competition in their private lives and in the nation's economic affairs are invariably those who start with a considerable advantage over their competitors. They see to it, in other words, that the competition is far from being equal. For their children's education this means private coaches and fee-paying schools; at the commercial level it means cartels and massive corporations which obliterate their rivals by sheer force of numbers.

The study of human societies reveals two broad principles which can be distinguished as providing the foundation for general social relationships. These are competition and co-operation. In some communities one is stressed rather than the other; in other communities there is a precarious balance between both, with co-operation always being emphasised at times of severe crisis. This suggests that co-operation is the more fundamental and indispensable bond. It is one we can choose to emphasise if we so desire while also confining competition to narrower and narrower areas of human experience. We could easily, for instance, retain competitiveness for sport and athletics while banishing it from education and industry. The choice, however, is ours. And this means that, in the final analysis, it is an individual choice. Each citizen must make a personal decision. In order to choose effectively he will need to have been educated in a particular way and to have grown up in a specific kind of community. *Laissez faire* or *laissez aller* will not do either as policies for economics and business or for morals and political life today or in the future.

2

In the field of education the ideas and values I have been emphasising imply the carrying out of a major revolution. They necessitate the fusion of the private and authority schools into one general system of education. This amalgamation would extend to include universities, training colleges and all academies of higher learning or professional training. Whatever the costs and possible losses, the widespread existence of private educational arrangements is intolerable and immoral. It cannot be supported on ethical grounds, only on grounds of personal expediency and individual competitiveness.

I am quite sure indeed that it is only a matter of time before the state primary schools in Britain as in America become the springboard for children of every class and social group. Recently a Tory Minister of Education went on record advocating the surprisingly socialistic policy of common primary education for all. And once that is achieved, the way to communal secondary schooling becomes more and more possible. We may indeed look forward to a time when secondary education is similar to University education which, at the moment, Oxbridge apart, knows few status distinctions.

I have no doubt that educational inequalities both in respect of content and duration and of academic status contribute powerfully to much adolescent unrest. In the older and poorer slum neighbourhoods there are often to be found what might be called 'pockets of anti-education' where both young and old, children and their parents, are either positively opposed to the work of the schools or, at best, passively submit to their statutory ministrations. Not surprisingly the pupils who leave such mediocre schools do poorly in competitive examinations. They possess little or no skill. They do not seek any form of further education in later life. They content themselves with the rewards of manual labour and follow tough but ultimately very unrewarding avenues of employment.

Unless we are very careful indeed one grave and unplanned result of the increasing scope and competitiveness of our expanding educational system will be that a minority of less favoured and possibly less able people will get left very far behind in the struggle for a higher standard of life. We may see the re-emergence of the nineteenth-century phenomenon of the Two Nations—two opposed and rapidly separating ways of living—confronting each other with mutual mistrust and misunderstanding. The recently published report of the Newsom Committee has drawn attention to this grave social and industrial danger.[1]

This phenomenon, which already appears to be observable in the United States, will result in the creation of what we may term permanently alienated social groups, bent on their own kind of achievement but living largely outside the limits of culturally acceptable bounds. The teenage gang, the band of youthful drug addicts, professional criminality and the cult of violence witness to

[1] *Half Our Future*, a Report of the Central Advisory Council for Education (England), H.M.S.O., 1963.

the gravity of the problems which are all boiling beneath the surface of law and order and which occasionally erupt.

In the educational sphere, the authorities should make a strenuous effort to eliminate these pathogenic inequalities. This means *inter alia* rebuilding the old city schools as a matter of top priority and also of experimenting with various projects aiming to link up school and home in a working partnership dedicated to the welfare of children and young people.

In the allied field of leisure time activities and recreation and in Further Education generally the authorities have an equally important task to perform. It is extraordinary how thin the provision for youth work and Further Education is in some parts of the country and in some parts of particular cities and towns. As far as the Youth Service goes, we have provision, at most, for no more than a third of the juvenile population. The whole business must therefore become selective. There is no sense, moreover, in bleating about the 'unattached' or bewailing the so-called 'unclubbables' until a place for everyone is made available within the framework of the existing youth organisations.

I would like to suggest here that we should treat the older teenagers in a rather different fashion from the ones who are still in fulltime attendance at school or who have only just started work. The concept of a youth centre, somewhat on the lines of the British Council centres in this country and overseas, where something of the atmosphere of a junior common room is created and fostered, where pure amusement, physical pursuits and educational programmes can be promoted under the same roof, and where opportunities for eating, dancing and other informal social activities also exist, has much to recommend itself. Every neighbourhood in fact should have its own students' union.

While older teenagers require less supervision and much more tutoring, the younger ones seem to profit most from the more orthodox kind of groups. But these groups usually fail to cater for the under-fourteens with the result that a great opportunity for making a contribution to the reduction of juvenile delinquency is constantly being missed.

3

In the modern world it is impossible to think of education in a vacuum. It is impossible to think of it apart from the neighbourhood influences and it is equally unrealistic to talk about it as something remote from the sphere of work. The last years of formal schooling, therefore, must be linked to the first years of gainful employment. There must be no sudden break with learning nor must we allow the sometimes fussy atmosphere of the classroom to obtrude into the workshop.

The final years of school life need to be much more relaxed and permissive than they often are.

Pari passu with this should go a more comradely relationship between teacher and pupil, less imposition of arbitrary discipline and a greater sense of sharing than has characterised British schools in the past.[1] Mr A. B. Clegg, Chief Education Officer of the West Riding of Yorkshire, in a most interesting enquiry carried out to discover what, if any, connection there was between the use of corporal punishment, the incidence of juvenile delinquency and good conduct in a sample of secondary schools in his area, showed that behaviour was best in schools which resorted least to caning.[2] He also showed that the influence of the head teacher could often prove crucial in determining the quality of a school's internal discipline and also of its external image. These findings, moreover, seem to be valid irrespective of the type of locality in which the schools are situated. The tougher and rougher neighbourhoods respond to a humane and sympathetic discipline every whit as well as better class districts.

The early years at work ought not to be completely divorced from the idea of extending knowledge and of widening intellectual or aesthetic experience. An honest acceptance of the vocational element in most education would help considerably and the idea of education for work as something desirable, rather than as a distasteful necessity thrust upon educators by a crudely materialistic community, should be much more widely accepted without sacrificing any elements of human worth and dignity.

But it is invidious to get the schools excited about industry and the pupils psychologically geared up to the factory ethos if, when schooldays are over, work is hard or impossible to come by. The necessity that faces us as a society is to find or provide suitable

[1] This is especially true during the last years of school life in both grammar and secondary modern schools in Britain.

[2] A brief account of this enquiry will be found in the *Education* pamphlet, *Delinquency and Discipline*, published by Councils and Education Press, 1963, in a section called 'The Role of the School', pp. 15–16.

employment for all school leavers in jobs which offer fair prospects and rewards and which, at the same time, make demands on them and are not an affront to their self-respect. Unsatisfactory work, or no work at all, can so easily lead to youthful demoralisation and consequent unrest and anti-social behaviour. This is, of course, more than a parochial or even a regional concern. It is a national problem which calls for the most careful and far-seeing planning of both human and physical resources.

Yet at the local, as well as at the national level, much might be done straight away with the existing services to give young people more help in the employment field. One thing we could try to do is to link the curriculum of the schools more closely with the needs and requirements of local industry and commerce. As I have already suggested, we should stop being so afraid of vocationalism in education. Potential employees must possess the necessary skills if new industries are to be attracted to any problem area. And one thing is certain, they will not be attracted if the educational level is low and if traditions of casual manual labour predominate in people's minds.

Day continuation classes of high calibre are a crying need at the moment. They might very well be linked up with the development of the County Colleges which were envisaged in the provisions of the 1944 Education Act but which, for economic and other reasons, have not yet been established. Some interesting experiments have been carried out in the country as a whole which point the way to future progress. For day continuation classes and County Colleges, providing part time education for youngsters in fulltime employment, seem alone to be capable of bridging this awkward transition between school and work. Moreover, they offer youngsters who have not made the best use of their school life a chance to make up for past deficiencies and lost opportunities. Here those young people who saw little purpose in what was offered them at school may find new motivation and come in time to bend themselves to the acquisition of new skills, and, even to the task of passing necessary examinations to give them access to trade or professional and commercial employment.

The whole concept of Youth Colleges (or whatever we choose to call them) functioning for young employees for one whole day a week with occasional voluntary evening activities of a recreative character seems to me most attractive—perhaps the one hopeful idea that has emerged in recent years to attempt to cope with some of the root causes of youthful disillusionment and consequent unrest. Such institutes, as I see them, would be a combination of a first-class youth club and technical college. Those attending them would be ranked as students not pupils. The teaching staff or tutors would need to be able, not only to instruct in a specific subject, but also equipped to discuss informatively, informally and sympathetically subjects as widely ranging as industrial relations, religious and philosophical problems, international affairs, and psychological and personality problems.

I am well aware of the immense difficulties which lie in the way of putting into effect the suggestions proposed in the preceding paragraphs.[1] Resources for such a venture would have to be made available nationally but local authorities meanwhile have a vital job to do in preparing the ground for the future establishment of such further educational colleges. This means creating a sound working relationship with employers and with industry (including the trade unions which we often overlook to our peril) and with voluntary associations as a necessary preliminary step. Industry and commerce must be linked actively to vocational guidance bodies and to the schools. Teachers, parents, youth leaders, industrial managers and trade union officials should be brought into a common endeavour to prevent young people losing their way in life and developing dangerous feelings of aimlessness and isolation. This must be done not merely to prevent crime or reduce social problems but out of a deep concern for people expressing itself in disinterested and compassionate social service.

Local authorities have the task, as far as the regional area is concerned, of seeing the problem of young people growing up in the round. Not only must they strive to bring about liaison between all interested parties at adult level, they must also make the whole thing live and attractive to the youngsters themselves.

Heartening news is coming in from the London area which suggests that much more can be done at the present moment to promote this kind of further educational service than is often supposed. Somehow it appears sites have been found and buildings

---

[1] One of which is, of course, the raising of the school leaving age in Britain to 16. This might prove to be in the end a less satisfactory way of dealing with youngsters from inner city neighbourhoods than the provision of county colleges.

equipped and the great adventure of Further Education got under way.[1]

A pioneer in this field is the County College at Childwall, Liverpool, which has been in existence now since 1954. There boys and girls from very mixed social backgrounds, many indeed from the older and poorer parts of the city, meet together on a voluntary basis but with the full support of their employers to increase their technical competence, to study for various examinations and for more general cultural pursuits in the way of drama, music, current affairs and handicrafts of all kinds. The results and, above all, the tone of the college, are most encouraging.[2]

It is clear that, even if we did have a widespread further educational service for all young people, say from the time they leave school until their eighteenth birthday, many problems would remain. Neither the generous provision of part-time colleges nor a vastly expanded and pepped up Youth Service would meet the needs of all young people. At the same time they would certainly help some youngsters to cope more successfully with the business of growing up and finding a way in the world.

As we saw in a preceding chapter the status of the young worker today needs to be substantially upgraded. The whole apprenticeship system cries aloud for government reformation but so far no government has had the courage and the positive vision to take a strong initiative in this sphere. More attention should be paid to the needs and to the future prospects of the average or slightly below average boys and girls who leave the secondary modern schools at the age of fifteen plus and who have little guidance or support in making a career for themselves.[3] The responsibility cannot in every case be thrust on to parental shoulders, nor can we always assume that the educational services are in a position to make good whatever deficiencies arise from a family's inability to cope adequately with its own work problems. The Youth Employment bureaux are, as we have seen, amongst the most frustrated of social welfare institutions for reasons connected with the ordering of society and not from any inherent lack of zeal on the part of individual counsellors.

We have to remember that the rapid changes which have occurred in Society in the past twenty years or so have borne most heavily

---

[1] See various L.C.C. Reports, e.g. *On From School*, for further details.

[2] I have already described this in detail in an earlier book. See *Education and the Urban Child*, pp. 160–77.   [3] Cf. *Half Our Future*, op. cit.

upon those social groups least equipped by experience or training
to deal with unfamiliar conditions. The social and educational élite
have experienced much less difficulty in adjusting to changes which,
in any case, involve no more than an extension of their own privileges
to wider sections of the community. But the products of working
class homes and working class cultural backgrounds have experienced the greater difficulties and evidenced, in their sometimes
alarming behaviour, symptoms of the stress generated by the widespread changes that have taken place since the last war. For these
youngsters, above all, we should heed the plea, put forward amongst
others by Dr Wall,[1] for an integrated educational service incorporating induction to work, technical training, vocational guidance
and the programmes of full-time, part-time and further education.
At the moment there are many gaps and deficiencies, many un-
manned loopholes in our defences. It is only too likely that when
an adolescent goes to work he is left without any sustaining adult
guidance at all, either from a sympathetic older workmate or from
some professionally equipped and responsible member of the firm.

The kind of Further Educational or County Colleges already
referred to in this chapter, however, offer one hopeful way in which
this kind of inter-generational culture-contact could be achieved.
At the more recreational and artistic level, moreover, the new
Midland Arts Centre recently set up in an Edgbaston park which
offers films, drama, dancing, the visual arts, and music together
with purely social and athletic activities suggests a useful model
which might well be developed in other parts of the country as an
ancillary service related to more formal educational methods.[2]

As far as guidance on personal problems associated with the new
experience of work goes, the young employees in some kinds of
employment and in larger firms do have the opportunity of contact
with the Appointed Factory Doctor who by law is required to see
them regularly from the time of their intake until their eighteenth
birthday.[3] A boy's first year in industry is one which is supremely
vital for the development of future attitudes towards work itself
and for the growth in understanding of the dignity of human labour.
All too often it is frittered away doing odd jobs and making tea with

1 Wall, *Child of Our Times*, op. cit., p. 99.
2 See Roy Shaw's report on this venture in *New Society*, No. 16, January,
1963, 'Blooms in the Desert?', p. 25.
3 For a full and illuminating account of the work of the A.F.D. see M. E. M.
Herford's *Youth at Work*, Max Parrish, London, 1954.

the result that the recruit tends to fall into bad habits and develops a resentful frame of mind. The service of the Appointed Factory Doctor (often a local G.P.) should be closely linked with the Youth Employment and School Medical services of the district and he should liaise with all other organisations catering for the under eighteens. More especially his services should be extended to all young people under the age of eighteen who are in fulltime employment and not, as at present, confined to those in certain large industries.

Such steps as these we have been discussing would go some way in the direction of righting what is wrong in contemporary youth culture. They would help to give to the children of ordinary families the support, guidance and encouragement which the offspring of more privileged groups have hitherto alone enjoyed. We can deal with adolescents by ignoring them, more or less as we do now, and by criticising them when they break what we consider to be bounds of decency. We can, like the Victorians, seek to rush young people into adulthood at the earliest possible moment and with the minimum of fuss. Or, on the other hand, we can accept youth as an inevitability, as an essential preparatory period between childhood and maturity which is afforded its own institutional care and is granted status in its own right. In other words we can accept the fact that teenagers not only must exist as a separate group but that they are also beneficial for society; that their transitional stage is not a public nuisance but a socially valuable growing point, and then act accordingly.

It is no use labelling all young people who fail to fit neatly into the prevailing mode delinquents or deviants. We have got to realise that the problems of youth are very much more than manifestations of adolescent intransigence. They are at least fifty per cent social problems—our problems, in other words. Young people cannot be expected to solve them for us by behaving a little better and by agreeing to kick over the traces less. Only the responsible adult generation has the power and the sophistication to do what is necessary. To do what is necessary means, amongst other things, radically reforming the entire educational system, not just with a view to eliminating injustices between individuals or creating a fairer meritocracy, but with the object of closing the gap between the intellectual élite and the culturally deprived. To achieve this, of course, would necessarily imply the creation of an entirely different kind of society than the one we now operate.

4

The argument thus returns from the specific to the general, from the practical to the philosophical. Because, in the last resort, there is nothing more practical than men's philosophical ideas. Whatever physical improvements our schools come to enjoy, whatever new procedures we invent for easing the transition from school to work, techniques of vocational guidance and sympathetic supervision during the early years in employment, whatever colleges and youth clubs we provide, all our efforts will stand or fall on the sincerity of our commitment to a new community life. This means a compassionate concern for individual persons at every stage of their lives. The two besetting youth problems, of delinquency on the one hand and over-conformity on the other, which we have been discussing, arise from the same root source. They derive from indifference and selfishness at all levels—parental, social and personal. If adolescence is to play its true functional role in society as the growing point of future development, we will have to find a way to implant into youngsters' minds moral ideas which will lead them to follow enthusiastically in the direction we believe that, as a society, we ought to go. Fear of indoctrination should not be allowed to dissuade us from our purpose. Parents, teachers, youth leaders, all who in any way or in any capacity come into vital contact with growing minds must be helped to take their full share in this essential training. This means that religious, ethical and political concepts and philosophies must be faced and dealt with all along the line.

With the passing of the era of widespread allegiance to organised religion, many people feel that there is little or nothing to be put in its place. Parents often leave it to the schools to give their children some philosophical teaching and to develop them ethically. For the most part parents and teachers, however, take society as it stands on its own terms. Only those with a strong sense of religious belief or political commitment take a positive line with their children and try to train them in a specific manner. Many, indeed, think that it is wrong to present children with positive moral ideas at all. They regard it as narrow-minded bullying, part of that Victorianism which has been thankfully left behind. Such an attitude seems to me to be seriously mistaken and socially menacing. If individuals are brought up without moral ideas and values it is hardly surprising that our social institutions, our national life and public affairs are similarly maintained in an atmosphere of easy-going, pleasure-seeking indifference. Where parents abdicate we are obliged to rely upon the schools and the youth organisations to do that part of their task for the sake of the children and, also, of course, for the sake of society.

Nowadays we set great store by professionalism and go in for a good deal of training. There is hope in this as well as potential danger. The hope is that those who are responsible for training the trainers, those whose task it is to teach the future teachers will be men and women of strong moral calibre, profound sympathy and compassionate concern for those who are the ultimate recipients of the service.

I hope not to be misunderstood here. I do not want to see the growth of a bureaucratised educational system or the creation of a national youth movement or an evangelical social army or anything of that sort. What I want to see is the people with power and responsibility for administration in society, especially in the educational field, taking responsibility for morality in addition to their other burdens. Society cannot survive without civilisation. We must achieve a civilised society or perish. There has to be moral consensus and moral direction and a serious commitment to ethical principles. These principles begin, I am convinced, in the individual heart and mind but, if society is to be regenerated, they must pass over into social organisation and inspire the social structure itself.

Youth possesses two sublime attributes: idealism and energy. It is the task of the older folk to provide the leadership and sense of direction. Growing minds can be seized with generous impulses. They can equally be conditioned to a self-centred hedonism. It is the unique responsibility of teachers, parents and youth workers to make the right appeal at the crucial stage of their development. And if I were asked what two ideas I would above all others seek to inculcate at this impressionable age I would choose these. First, that the human mind, spirit, soul (whatever you call it seems unimportant) can rise above all adversities, and second that individual moral choices count in the sum total of things. These two truths seem to be of paramount importance for the future of our culture and our race. But they are, as I am well aware, ones which would be disputed by many people today. Some, with regret, would claim that we are impotent victims of forces outside our control. Others would dismiss my propositions on materialistic philosophical grounds, while yet again there might well be those gloomy existentialists who see the human condition as irretrievably ruinous and irredeemable.

For Christians, of course, there is less argument. They know that man is a moral being and they know that personal decisions are indeed decisive. The trouble with the Christian Church, however, is that it has spent far too much time worrying about what happens after death, about doctrines of redemption and ideas of retribution. It has not concerned itself, certainly for a very long time, with what is going on here and now in this world and in society. The individual has been encouraged to be especially concerned about his own salvation rather than with the redemption of society.

But our concern here is more with the non-Christians, with those who find the metaphysics unacceptable and who, wrongly in my opinion, believe themselves to be spiritually adrift. They can find meaning in life to hand on to the rising generation if they cast around for it. It is a meaning of which they need not feel ashamed; a similar meaning in fact to the one that the Christians avow, although they arrive at it from another direction, and base their allegiance upon humanistic foundations.

That a man can die spiritually triumphant in the teeth of apparent defeat is the great lesson for which there are many exemplars even in our own day and age. Those who withstood the Nazi assault on mind and body although dying in the concentration and extermination camps testify to the same truth; that some can prevail against the most dastardly assaults without losing their integrity. In other words, the individual is crucial: his will power, vision and strength determine the nature and course of civilisation. The ethics he chooses to adopt become in time those of society as a whole and if they are based upon reverence for life and concern for the welfare of persons —whatever the state of a man's metaphysical or theological belief, all will be well.

What I am claiming is that there is a religious truth which is sustained even though some of the religious ideas which have been associated with it are no longer tenable.

I believe that it is our duty to put before young people examples of lives which have been lived at a level of sublimity (lives which are themselves revelations) and which have most conspicuously not been failures, and examples, too, of lives lived at a pitch of altruistic self-giving that command our unhesitating worship. They show what can be done, that the human spirit can triumph over everything. Even though the vast majority of us are weak and selfish and contemptible creatures, we can know what is possible to choicer spirits. While they are remembered there need be no lack of substance to our ethical teaching.

5

The business of sexual behaviour is very properly an educational and a moral topic. People's attitudes towards sexual behaviour are related to their attitudes towards other aspects of human experience and subject to the same cultural pressures as any other part of their lives. Preparation for marriage, or, at least, for sexuality, is part and parcel of the educational process if by education we mean a preparation of the individual to lead a full and happy adult life. We will do young people a great disservice in this sector of their lives if we tell them that sexual experience is altogether outside their control, that it cannot be submitted to the authority of the will, or, worse, that to submit it to such control exerts untold physical and psychological harm. The image of the happy home is one which is constantly being pushed in front of young people's noses by commercial and advertising agencies who want to sell more refrigerators or more do-it-yourself paraphernalia. It is by no means an entirely erroneous image but it does often give only the most superficial impression of what is entailed in marriage, family life and home-making. Discussions with people who have special knowledge and with ordinary folk who have firsthand experience are very desirable at school, youth club and county college. Young people almost everywhere, today as ever, are starved of sensible conversation. They lack opportunities to talk freely and confidentially with older people who have had more experience of life than themselves. But formal education spends little time on such issues. It tends to ignore the deep and significant things in life and passes them by in an embarrassed silence, or, if it deals with them at all, it is superficially, conventionally and in an authoritarian atmosphere. Religious instruction in schools, indeed, often begs honest questions and evades reasonable doubt. There is surely something drastically amiss with our much vaunted education if it contents itself with imparting knowledge about things and events, mathematical formulae and theories of natural science, yet rapidly skates over the far more serious and vital questions of human ethics and human destiny.

Education—formal and informal—is the responsibility of the whole community. The bringing up and training of youth is thus a community task. If it is usually performed for us by specialists this does not absolve us from responsibility for what they do and what the outcome of their efforts proves to be. The community must accept this charge and see to it that (a) the institutions provided are adequate to the task and (b) the people who perform it are aware of what is expected of them. The quality of social life depends to a considerable degree on our educational institutions. These in turn, depend absolutely on the values which we as a community hold to be fundamental for our present stability and future survival. Moral considerations are hence basic to the whole process. And because we nowadays are often divided about these moral principles, difficulties and problems arise in the social sphere. Young people react most sensitively to these dilemmas and their sometimes disturbed behaviour witnesses to the importance of a social consensus being reached.

The first task, therefore, in dealing with the so-called youth problem is for those in authority and those of an age to have a voice in the affairs of society to reach agreement on what kind of society we want to live in. This is so vast a subject in itself that I will not here embark on answering the question, how is this to be done? I will merely assume that it can be done, that in the past, to some extent anyway, it has happened, not so much as a result of free democratic choice as of a policy of traditionalism, drift and raw expediency combined, and that in the future it can be brought more under the control of conscious and rational choice.

When we are clearer on our own moral grounds we can then turn our attention to the business of training youth so that they have an honoured place in the social order and are given a realistic role in life. In contemporary U.S.A., from all reports, youth is being pushed further and further into the margins of social life, being given an increasingly frivolous and protracted waiting role to perform, with a result that young people there have sought to create their own specific youth culture out of sheer social desperation. In Britain things have not yet come to such a pass, but there are signs that we may be going to repeat transatlantic experiences in this as in many other departments of our national life. We have still an opportunity to avoid this happening over here however.

What we have to do is to take positive social action to make adolescence a definite stage in social development. Middle and upper class youth have long enjoyed the specific youth culture provided for them by boarding or grammar school and university. They accepted it all, on the whole peaceably, because of the high status attached to this form of education and because of the tempting future that awaited them at the end of the adolescent road. But for the vast majority of young people no such culturally ordered development existed. Working class youngsters have been left very much to the mercy of the market-place and chance. The kind of comprehensive programme of training which we have been discussing in the preceding pages would be designed to avoid precisely this. It would aim to give all youth, including those of lesser ability and those from less prosperous backgrounds, a genuine stake in society. It would seek to provide acceptable educative influences outside, but closely linked with, the formal teaching institutions which would be available, at least, until a young person attained the age of eighteen. Guidance, support, encouragement should be provided at every stage of the road. Above all there must be no patronage and no authoritarianism in the social climate of the institutions serving youth.

The eighteenth birthday might well be regarded as the high water mark of youth and the time when adult status could safely be given. It could usefully be the time when legal status is attained, when the franchise is enjoyed and the full responsibilities of maturity assumed.[1] It proved a more or less viable age for military service to begin and there is no good reason, especially in view of the fact that maturity may now be being reached at a somewhat earlier date than heretofore, why we should cling to the traditional twenty-first birthday as the moment when full citizenship is conferred. We simply must take into consideration the fact that by the late teens many young men and many more young women are married and some are indeed already parents. This trend is one that we have no alternative but to accept, and if we can come to accept it with enthusiasm and optimism rather than with dismay and despair so much the better for us all. Indeed, the growing popularity of marriage amongst the young

---

[1] There are grounds, too, for making eighteen the age of legal consent, too, i.e., the age by which it is considered reasonable for youngsters to agree to entering into sexual relations.

may itself be an indication of their keen desire to escape as soon as possible from a position of indeterminate status.

If we seek to promote in young people a condition of emotional and of allied intellectual sincerity these qualities must also be incorporated in our own attitudes and approach to them. Courage, absence of false shame, fearless integrity and determination to deal justly with one another should be the ideals of the school, the college and the youth club. They must be much more widely achieved in the future if these youth-serving organisations are to prosper and perform their essential function adequately. But they cannot do this in the teeth of social inequalities, ingrained class discrimination and organised dishonesty. We must work on the social structure itself as well as with the personalities of young people if we wish to bring about a substantial change in the relationship between the generations and reduce the degree of antagonism and misunderstanding which too often characterise relations today. Young people are especially subject, as research has repeatedly shown, to the influence of the home and to members of the peer group. If, by working on parents and peers, our educative institutions succeed in establishing a better relationship between youth and the rest of society, a useful beginning will have been made towards solving some of the problems of delinquency, violence and moral non-commitment which afflict the community today and which are a real threat to the future. But these reforms can be severely frustrated by our economic, commercial, political and public life, some aspects of which are clearly not in harmony with the educational ideals we have outlined and few of which seem consciously to be shaped in conformity with any obvious ethical code. Youth can be led to criticise existing arrangements and assumptions and fired with an enthusiasm to change things when they come into power, but it is idle to imagine that this will generate enough dynamism to produce all the reforms we require. Political action which incorporates the group will and desire for a more ethical social order is unavoidable. Too often we are inclined to leave political action out of account entirely in our deliberations on social problems. We think that new schools and educational reforms of one kind or another or that the provision of fresh social amenities will do the trick for us. But we are invariably proved wrong. If we truly want a new quality of community life, then we must work for it and organise it. Moral attitudes, ethical values do not exist in a vacuum. They are inextricably interwoven with the social structure. Education, by itself, will not bring into being the kind of community we want or ensure the quality of relationships we yearn for unless the ideals of education are also supported by the other social institutions.

It is within the framework of this wider social context that the so-called problems of youth are to be understood and interpreted. Not until youth is given an adequate and assured place in the community will any substantial change in the desired direction be likely to occur.

SELECTED BIBLIOGRAPHY

ABRAMS, MARK. *The Teenage Consumer*. London: The London Press Exchange Ltd., 1959.

———. *The Teenage Consumer (part II)*. London: The London Press Exchange Ltd., 1961.

BARNES, L. J. *The Outlook for Youth Work*. London: King George's Jubilee Trust, 1948.

BEDNARIK, KARL. *The Young Worker of Today: A New Type*. New York: Free Press, 1956; London: Faber and Faber, 1953.

BLOS, PETER. *On Adolescence*. New York: Free Press, 1962.

BREW, J. MACALISTER. *In the Service of Youth*. London: Faber and Faber, 1943.

———. *Informal Education*. London: Faber and Faber, 1946.

———. *Youth and Youth Groups*. London: Faber and Faber, 1957.

CARTER, M. P. *Home, School and Work*. New York: Pergamon Press, 1962.

COHEN, ALBERT. *Delinquent Boys*. New York: Free Press, 1955; London: Routledge and Kegan Paul, 1956.

COLEMAN, JAMES S. *The Adolescent Society*. New York: Free Press, 1961.

EISENSTADT, S. N. *From Generation to Generation*. New York: Free Press, 1955; London: Routledge and Kegan Paul, 1956.

ERIKSON, ERIK H. *Childhood and Society*. New York: Norton, 1964; London: Imago.

FERGUSON, T., and CUNNISON, J. *The Young Wage-Earner*. New York and London: Oxford University Press, 1951.

———. *In Their Early Twenties*. London: Oxford University Press, 1956.

FLEMING, C. M. *Adolescence, Its Social Psychology*. 2nd ed. revised. New York: Humanities Press; London: Routledge and Kegan Paul, 1963.

FRIEDENBERG, EDGAR Z. *The Vanishing Adolescent*. New York: Dell/Laurel Books, 1962.

FYVEL, T. R. *The Insecure Offenders*. London: Chatto and Windus, 1961. In U.S.A.: *Troublemakers*. New York: Schocken Books.

HAVIGHURST, R. J. *Human Development and Education.* New York: McKay; London: Longmans, 1953.

——, *et al. Growing Up in River City.* New York: Wiley, 1962.

HEMMING, J. *Problems of Adolescent Girls.* London: Heinemann, 1960.

HERFORD, M. E. M. *Youth at Work.* London: Max Parrish, 1956.

HIGGINSON, M. *Learning and Living, A Feminine Viewpoint.* Bolton School Old Girls' Association, n.d.

HOGGART, RICHARD. *The Uses of Literacy.* Boston: Beacon Press, 1961; London: Chatto and Windus, 1957.

HOLLINGSHEAD, A. B. *Elmtown's Youth.* New York: Wiley, Science Editions, 1961.

JACKSON, B. and MARSDEN, D. *Education and the Working Class.* New York: Monthly Review Press; London: Routledge and Kegan Paul, 1962.

JEPHCOT, P. *Girls Growing Up.* London: Faber and Faber, 1942.

——. *Some Young People.* London: Allen and Unwin, 1954.

JORDAN, G. W., and FISHER, E. M. *Self-Portrait of Youth.* London: Heinemann, 1955.

MAYS, J. B. *Growing Up in the City.* New York: Lounz, 1959; Liverpool: Liverpool University Press, 1964.

——. *Education and the Urban Child.* New York: Lounz, 1960; Liverpool: Liverpool University Press, 1962.

MEAD, MARGARET. *Growing Up in New Guinea.* Gloucester, Massachusetts: Peter Smith; Harmondsworth: Penguin Books, 1942.

——. *Coming of Age in Samoa.* Gloucester, Massachusetts: Peter Smith; Harmondsworth: Penguin Books, 1954.

MORGAN, A. E. *Young Citizen.* Harmondsworth: Penguin Books, 1943.

MORSE, MARY. *The Unattached.* Harmondsworth: Penguin Books, 1965.

PETERSON, A. D. C. *Educating Our Rulers.* London: Duckworth, 1957.

REED, BRYAN. *Eighty Thousand Adolescents.* London: Allen and Unwin, 1950.

SALISBURY, HARRISON. *The Shook-Up Generation.* New York: Harper and Row, 1958; London: Michael Joseph, 1959.

SIMEY, T. S. *The Concept of Love in Child Care.* London: Oxford University Press, 1961.

SMITH, ERNEST A. *American Youth Culture, Group Life in Teenage Society.* New York: Free Press, 1962.

TANNER, J. M. *Growth at Adolescence.* Philadelphia: Davis, 1961; London: Blackwell, 1955.

TAWNEY, R. H. *The Acquisitive Society.* Gloucester, Massachusetts: Peter Smith; London: Fontana Books, 1961.

VALENTINE, C. W. *The Normal Child.* Harmondsworth: Penguin Books, 1956.

VENESS, THELMA. *School Leavers.* New York: Humanities Press; London: Methuen, 1962.

WALL, W. D. *Education and Mental Health.* London: UNESCO/ Harrap, 1955.

————. *Child of Our Times.* London: National Children's Home, 1959.

WILKINS, LESLIE T. *The Adolescent in Britain.* London: Central Office of Information, 1955.

WILLIAMS, GERTRUDE. *Recruitment to Skilled Trades.* New York: Humanities Press; London: Routledge and Kegan Paul, 1957.

————. *Training for Skill.* Fabian Research Pamphlet No. 205, 1959.

WILLIAMS, RAYMOND. *Culture and Society, 1780–1950.* New York: Harper and Row; London: Chatto and Windus, 1958.

YABLONSKY, LEWIS. *The Violent Gang.* New York: Macmillan, 1962.

Reports

The Youth Service in England and Wales, Report of the Albemarle Committee, Cmnd. 929, H.M.S.O., 1960.

15 to 18, Report of the Central Advisory Council for Education (England), H.M.S.O., 1959.

Half Our Future, Report of the Central Advisory Council for Education (England), H.M.S.O., 1963.

Citizens of Tomorrow, A Study of the Influences Affecting the Upbringing of Young People, King George's Jubilee Trust, 1955.

Spontaneous Youth Groups, University of Bristol Institute of Education Publication No. 8, University of London Press, 1955.

Teenage Morals, Councils and Education Press Ltd., 1961.

Delinquency and Discipline, Councils and Education Press Ltd., 1962.

Teenage Culture, Annals of the American Academy of Political and Social Science, November, 1961.

Training For Skill, Report of a Sub-Committee of the National Joint Advisory Council, H.M.S.O., 1958.

Teddy Boys and Teddy Girls, International Child Welfare Review, Vol. XV, No. 4, 1961.

School and Social Maladjustment of Youth, Report of a meeting of experts, U.N.E.S.C.O. Youth Institute, Gauting/München, 1960.

Local Authorities and Youth Problems, International Union of Local Authorities, Special Series No. 7, The Hague, 1963.

INDEX